MW01294033

JOSHUA

H. A. IRONSIDE

An Ironside Expository Commentary

JOSHUA

H. A. IRONSIDE

Kregel
Academic & Professional

Joshua: An Ironside Expository Commentary

Originally published in 1950. Reprinted in 2008 by Kregel Publications, a division of Kregel, Inc., P.O. Box 2607, Grand Rapids, MI 49501.

All Scripture quotations, unless otherwise indicated, are from the King James Version of the Holy Bible.

ISBN 978-0-8254-2927-9

Printed in the United States of America

08 09 10 11 12 / 5 4 3 2 1

CONTENTS

PREFACE

The present series of addresses on the book of Joshua consists of stenographic notes, somewhat abbreviated, covering messages that I gave on consecutive Lord's days at the Moody Memorial Church in Chicago.

At the request of many they are now sent forth in book form, in the hope that they may prove helpful and edifying to those who will take time to peruse them.

—H. A. IRONSIDE

CHAPTER 1

THE DIVINELY APPOINTED LEADER

Joshua 1:1–9

Now after the death of Moses the servant of the LORD it came to pass, that the LORD spake unto Joshua the son of Nun, Moses' minister, saying, Moses my servant is dead; now therefore arise, go over this Jordan, thou, and all this people, unto the land which I do give to them, even to the children of Israel. Every place that the sole of your foot shall tread upon, that have I given unto you, as I said unto Moses. From the wilderness and this Lebanon even unto the great river, the river Euphrates, all the land of the Hittites, and unto the great sea toward the going down of the sun, shall be your coast. There shall not any man be able to stand before thee all the days of thy life: as I was with Moses, so I will be with thee: I will not fail thee, nor forsake thee. Be strong and of a good courage: for unto this people shalt thou divide for an inheritance the land, which I sware unto their fathers to give them. Only be thou strong and very courageous, that thou mayest observe to do according to all the law, which Moses my servant commanded thee: turn not from it to the right hand or to the left, that thou mayest prosper whithersoever thou goest. This book of the law shall not depart out of thy mouth; but thou shalt meditate therein day and night, that thou mayest observe to do according to all that is written therein: for then thou shalt make thy way prosperous, and then thou shalt have good success. Have not I commanded thee? Be strong and of a good courage; be not afraid, neither be thou dismayed: for the LORD thy God is with thee whithersoever thou goest. (vv. 1–9)

The book of Joshua is distinctly the book of the inheritance and links very intimately with the epistle to the Ephesians in the New Testament. We have the manifestation of divine life in the book of Genesis; redemption in the book of Exodus; then the entrance into the holiest and the believer's sanctification typically set forth in Leviticus; the people of God under trial and testing in Numbers; and the government of God in Deuteronomy. Then we naturally move right on to the book of Joshua, in which we have the people of the Lord entering upon their inheritance.

In 1 Corinthians 10:11 we read that these things happened unto them for our types. So we are warranted to think of the land of Canaan as a type of the present blessings that are ours in Christ and to see in the wars of Israel a picture of the Christian's conflict. Israel's inheritance was of an earthly character. We might say they were blessed with all temporal blessings in earthly places in the land of Canaan. We, according to the epistle to the Ephesians, are blessed with all spiritual blessings in heavenly places in Christ.

As we open this book we are introduced to the divinely appointed leader who is to guide the people into their inheritance. It is very significant that the name "Joshua" is the same as the name that our blessed Lord bore here on earth. *Jesus* is the anglicized Greek form of *Joshua*. The word *Joshua* means "Jehovah the Savior," and we may see in this Joshua of the Old Testament a type of the Jesus of the New Testament. Moses, the lawgiver, led the people to the very border of the land but was not permitted to lead them into it. Joshua took up where Moses left off. The apostle Paul tells us that the law was Israel's child leader till Christ, but when Christ came they were no longer under the child leader. So we have in type the dispensation of the law passing away and the new dispensation of grace beginning. Of course, the people were actually under the law during all the days of Joshua and the Old Testament, and during the time of our Lord's earthly ministry. It was not until the Lord's resurrection that believers were delivered from the law. Joshua typifies the risen One leading us on into the privileges of the new creation.

We read first of the death of Moses. "Now after the death of Moses the servant of the LORD it came to pass, that the LORD spake unto Joshua the son of Nun, Moses' minister." This was when Israel was encamped east of the Jordan in the land of Moab. The Jordan was the eastern border of that part of the land separating Palestine from Moab. At God's command Moses went up to the top of Mount

Nebo and viewed the land and there died. The Lord Himself, we are told, buried him and no one knows where his sepulcher is to this day. Moses was so anxious to go into the land. He pleaded with the Lord to permit it, but he had failed at the water of Meribah, and God told him he could not enter Canaan. Moses prayed earnestly to be allowed to go in. Finally, God said, "Speak to Me no more about this matter." But He told him he could view the land from the top of Mount Nebo. Moses got into the land eventually when on the Mount of Transfiguration he and Elijah appeared with the Lord Jesus, and they were speaking of those things which should shortly be accomplished at Jerusalem—the work of the cross which our Savior was just about to consummate.

When Moses died God put Joshua in his place. He was to lead the people into their inheritance. The Lord had promised the land to them long before; He gave it to them by title. Now He says very definitely, "Moses my servant is dead; now therefore arise, go over this Jordan, thou, and all this people, unto the land which I do give to them, even to the children of Israel. Every place that the sole of your foot shall tread upon, that have I given unto you, as I said unto Moses."

It is one thing to have title to an inheritance, but it is quite another thing to make it one's own practically. We who are saved are blessed with all spiritual blessings in heavenly places in Christ, but how much of our inheritance have we actually appropriated? How much do you really enjoy of that which is yours in Christ? Many of us live in doubt, trouble, and perplexity most of the time. We fail to enter into and enjoy that which God has given us in His Son.

I have often likened this to a library. People sometimes come into my little study and look about. I have a few books which I have accumulated in the course of fifty years, perhaps some three thousand or more, and some people who are not used to doing much reading think that I have quite a collection. There are not nearly as many as there would be if a lot of my friends would return borrowed books. Sir Walter Scott once called those people, "Good bookkeepers."

But some folks look around and ask, "Do all these books belong to you?"

I say, "Yes, they are all mine." And I wish some other people could say the same thing about all the books they have!

The next question they ask is, "Have you read them all?"

I reply that I have read all that are worth reading. Sometimes I just get started and find that the book is worthless, so I do not finish it.

Well, the next question will be, "Do you know all that is in them?"

And I have to say, "No, I certainly do not. This little head of mine is much too small to contain all that is in these books."

Now our possessions in Christ are like that. The entire library is mine, but I do not really possess it. God has given us an inheritance, but we do not appropriate all that is ours.

Notice the extent of Israel's inheritance. "From the wilderness and this Lebanon even unto the great river, the river Euphrates, all the land of the Hittites, and unto the great sea toward the going down of the sun, shall be your coast." That took in the land from Euphrates down to the border of the land of Egypt, and the Mediterranean Sea, and then from the desert of Arabia on the south to Damascus on the north. God gave all this to Israel; and for a very brief time during Solomon's reign they possessed most of it, but they have never actually possessed for themselves all the land to which they were entitled. Some day they will. We are told in one of the Minor Prophets (Obad. 17) that the house of Israel shall possess their possessions. Oh, I wish that we as Christians might possess our possessions, and so enjoy the riches of our inheritance!

Just what do you mean by that, you ask? I mean, God has given us His Word. In this Word He has put before us our inheritance. He would have us study His Word, make it our own; enter into everything that it reveals. If we did this we would be able always to live a victorious life in Christ; we would really enjoy our inheritance in Him. Instead of dillydallying with the things of this poor world we would find something so much better in Him. A young man, after his conversion, was asked by some former friends of his to go to a movie. "No," he replied, "thanks, but I have no time; all my time is filled with the things of Christ." That is what it means to be delivered from the things of the world.

"There shall not any man be able to stand before thee all the days of thy life: as I was with Moses, so I will be with thee: I will not fail thee, nor forsake thee." God said, "You will not have to turn back; I'll drive out your foe before you." Alas, alas, they did not believe God's Word, and again and again the enemy reigned over them because of their own disobedience.

Now we wrestle not with flesh and blood; we are not engaged in a conflict with other nations. But our foes are spiritual, and the same God who fought for the people of Israel is the One who will give victory while we obey Him. We sing sometimes

Trust and obey, for there's no other way
To be happy in Jesus, But to trust and obey.
—John H. Sammis
"Trust and Obey"

In the next verse we have a word of encouragement. "Be strong and of a good courage: for unto this people shalt thou divide for an inheritance the land, which I sware unto their fathers to give them." We may take these words home to our hearts today when we are fearful of our spiritual foes.

"Only be thou strong and very courageous, that thou mayest observe to do according to all the law, which Moses my servant commanded thee: turn not from it to the right hand or to the left, that thou mayest prosper whithersoever thou goest." Victory depended on their adherence to the Word of God, and it is just as true today. We have so much more of God's Word than they had. They had only the five books of Moses and possibly the book of Job, which may have been written at that time. This is all the Bible they had, and God said, "Take this Word and walk in obedience to it, and you won't need to fear any foe; I'll ever be with you."

Now we have the whole Bible, and God calls upon us to search this Word; let it be the man of our counsel, the food of our souls, and the sword with which we face the enemy. God promises that if you will be strong and of a good courage and walk in obedience to His Word you will never need to dread the conflict; you will never need to fear; you will be able, at all times, to say with the apostle Paul, "Thanks be to God, which giveth us the victory through our Lord Jesus Christ" (1 Cor. 15:57).

If you do not have victory through Christ Jesus, I can tell you why. It is because you are neglecting reading and obeying your Bible. Read your Bible as you ought to and obey it, and you will be able to live a life of victory. John Bunyan had written in the front of his Bible, on the flyleaf, "This Book will keep you from sin or sin will keep you from this Book." We have the Scriptures to read, and we are to walk in obedience to the Word as it is opened to us by the Holy Spirit.

Young people, if you want to know what will make your life prosperous, get God's own recipe for good success. "This book of the law shall not depart out of thy mouth; but thou shalt meditate therein day and night, that thou mayest observe to do according to all that is written therein: for then thou shalt make thy way prosperous, and then thou shalt have good success." There you have it. Do you want your life to be prosperous? Do you want a successful career? Then take God's Word, read it, and obey it, and God promises those two things.

"Have not I commanded thee? Be strong and of a good courage; be not afraid, neither be thou dismayed: for the LORD thy God is with thee whithersoever thou goest." There seemed good reason why they should be afraid—unused to warfare as they were, facing seven nations with walled cities and armies, nations that had been constantly quarreling with each other down through the centuries, and the people of Israel were to go against these nations and take possession of their land. They might well tremble if they thought only of their own power and their own ability. But as they walked in obedience to the Word of the Lord He promised to deal with the enemies and to empower Israel to overcome them. Although we belong to a different dispensation we may take these words as an exhortation delivered to us personally, and as we read them and walk in obedience, we can count on God for victory.

Joshua was commanded not only to read but to meditate on the law of God. It is by meditation that we really make the Word our own. To read attentively is like eating the Word. Meditation answers to digestion of the truth. Mere intellectual acquaintance with the letter of Scripture avails little. It is as we weigh carefully what God has revealed that we obtain from it that spiritual power that enables us to rise above our difficulties and triumph by grace over all our foes. Thus we grow in grace and in the knowledge of our Lord Jesus Christ.

We become weak and are easily overcome when we neglect this important spiritual exercise, for the Word fed upon alone gives strength.

CHAPTER 2

PREPARATION FOR THE INHERITANCE

Joshua 1:10–18

Then Joshua commanded the officers of the people, saying, Pass through the host, and command the people, saying, Prepare you victuals; for within three days ye shall pass over this Jordan, to go in to possess the land, which the LORD your God giveth you to possess it. And to the Reubenites, and to the Gadites, and to half the tribe of Manasseh, spake Joshua, saying, Remember the word which Moses the servant of the LORD commanded you, saying, The LORD your God hath given you rest, and hath given you this land. Your wives, your little ones, and your cattle, shall remain in the land which Moses gave you on this side Jordan; but ye shall pass before your brethren armed, all the mighty men of valour, and help them; until the LORD have given your brethren rest, as he hath given you, and they also have possessed the land which the LORD your God giveth them: then ye shall return unto the land of your possession, and enjoy it, which Moses the LORD's servant gave you on this side Jordan toward the sunrising. And they answered Joshua, saying, All that thou commandest us we will do, and whithersoever thou sendest us, we will go. According as we hearkened unto Moses in all things, so will we hearken unto thee: only the LORD thy God be with thee, as he was with Moses. Whosoever he be that doth rebel against thy commandment, and will not hearken unto thy words in all that thou commandest him, he shall be put to death: only be strong and of a good courage. (vv. 10–18)

Israel had a long period of wandering in the wilderness. They were forty years making their way to the land of Canaan, and yet it could have been made in eleven days. But God led them about by way of the wilderness lest they should be discouraged if they immediately came in contact with their enemies. They journeyed during the first two years from Egypt to Kadesh-barnea, which was on the southwestern edge of the land, and from it they might have gone right up into their inheritance and taken possession of it. But you remember that at the request of the people, the Lord permitted Moses to send out spies in order to find out whether God was as good as His word! He had told them exactly what kind of land it was—a land flowing with milk and honey; but the people requested Moses to send spies to see what it was actually like, and he selected twelve men who went throughout all Palestine investigating. When they returned, ten of them reported that the land was everything God had said it was. "But," they added, "we never will be able to overcome the nations that dwell there. They are stronger than we; their cities are walled up to heaven; and there we saw the giants: and we were in their sight as grasshoppers, and so we were in our own sight. We are not able to go against them" (see Num. 13:28). Only two of the men encouraged the people. They were Joshua and Caleb. They said, "Let us go up at once and possess it; for we are well able to overcome it" (Num. 13:30). But the people would not believe them. So the Lord turned them back and they were destined to wander in the wilderness for thirty-eight years because they did not believe God. They refused to do as He had directed them. But He did not forsake them; He watched over them and protected them during all the years of their wilderness wanderings.

The people at last were encamped on the east of the Jordan, looking over toward Jericho. Then the word of God came to Joshua, saying, "Pass through the host, and command the people, saying, Prepare you victuals; for within three days ye shall pass over this Jordan, to go in to possess the land, which the LORD your God giveth you to possess it."

This land is typical of what we have in Christ. God "hath blessed us with all spiritual blessings in heavenly places in Christ." Yet we can possess our inheritance only as we recognize our death and resurrection with our Lord Jesus Christ. God had told Israel long before when in Egypt that they were to go three days' journey into the wilderness, which speaks of death and resurrection. Now the people of Israel were to go over Jordan in three days.

I wonder how far you and I have entered into our possessions in Christ. Many of us have come to Him as poor, needy sinners, and have trusted Him as our Savior, but are we now identified with Him in His death, burial, and resurrection? In God's reckoning every believer has been raised again with Christ. You remember what the apostle Paul said, "God forbid that I should glory, save in the cross of our Lord Jesus Christ, by whom the world is crucified unto me, and I unto the world" (Gal. 6:14). It is only as we take this place of identification with Christ practically that we enter into and enjoy our present inheritance in Him. It is the Word of God that brings these truths before us. Do we meditate upon the Word? Do we appropriate its precious truths? Do we feed our souls upon the blessed realities therein revealed? We would not think of going without our regular meals from day to day, but how many of us go without spiritual food! We cannot depend on another ministering to us; we must study the Word for ourselves. One who does not give time daily to meditation on the Word and to waiting on God in prayer will never be a strong Christian; he will never lay hold of that which the Lord intends him to enjoy as he is linked up with a risen Christ.

Well, Joshua here commands the people to prepare victuals for a three days' journey. They are to pass over Jordan right against Jericho. But first we notice that there is a particular group to whom he gives a special message. This group was made up of two and a half tribes—the Reubenites, Gadites, and half the tribe of Manasseh. Why did Joshua address himself to these tribes particularly? Well, for this reason: You remember how Israel under Moses overcame their foes on the east side of the Jordan, and the men of Reuben,

Gad, and half the tribe of Manasseh came to Moses, and they said, "This is a wonderful land, a great land for cattle, marvelous pastures here on the east side of Jordan, and we have cattle; therefore, we have come to ask if we might not have our inheritance here in this land instead of going over the Jordan. May we not settle here where we can find suitable accommodation?" Moses was very angry with them, and said, "Your brethren have to pass over the Jordan and they have to meet the seven nations, mightier and greater than they are; they have to overcome the enemies before they can have their inheritance and enjoy the land, yet you would settle down on the east side of Jordan in rest and freedom." But the tribes said, "No, we don't want to do that. We are willing to send our warriors over the Jordan to fight with the rest, but when at last they have obtained their land and have discomfited their foes, then our warriors will return to this side of Jordan. Meantime, we will arrange to make our wives and children comfortable in the cities on the east side, and we will make proper preparation for the care of our cattle, etc." Finally, Moses agreed to this. Sometimes God allows His people to take second best if they are not willing to take His best. Too many Christians today have been saved by grace but are content to settle down, as it were, on the east of Jordan. They have trusted Christ; they have heard the voice of God when He said, "When I see the blood I will pass over you," and they have come to the verge of Jordan, but they have missed many blessings because they have stopped on the east side. In other words, they are world-bordering Christians. These two and a half tribes settled in the land just bordering Canaan, and they were exposed to the nations of the east, to Assyria, Babylon, and the other countries roundabout. They were the first to be attacked by the enemies outside the land, who came down upon Israel in later times.

Let us ask our own hearts, "What kind of a Christian am I—out-and-out for God, or am I dwelling on the border of the world?" God made a dry way through Jordan for His people, and He has made a dry way through death for us today. We died with Christ at Calvary when He died in our place. There we were crucified with Him. Is this a reality to our souls? When Christians come to me and ask if there is any harm in this and that, something that pertains to the east side of Jordan, something in which the world indulges, I say, "Why don't you ask if there would be any harm in going to a prayer meeting?"

"Oh," they answer, "anybody knows there is no harm in going to a prayer meeting." Well, that is the answer. They would not think of asking the question if there was not a doubt in their minds. It is things like that of which the apostle speaks when he says that he that doubteth is condemned if he does the thing concerning which he is in doubt.

As to something of which you stand in doubt, you may be sure it will never help you spiritually; it will never help to make Christ more precious to you; it will never make you love His Word more; it will never enable you to triumph over sin. A great many of these things may not be wicked but are just bordering on the edge of the world, as it were. Like these two and a half tribes, you are settling down on the east side of Jordan. You have not gone through death, burial, and resurrection with Christ experimentally. Some have made a profession of this in Christian baptism, but are not living it out from day to day. In this ordinance we confess that we have died to the world, to sin, and to the law, and that we now are to live unto God as those who are alive from the dead. May our profession and our lives agree that the Lord Jesus may be magnified in us!

After Joshua's address to the two-and-a-half tribes who were to cross over the river to aid their brethren in taking possession of the inheritance, proceedings went on apace for the actual entering into that land which belonged already to Israel by divine gift, but which they were responsible to make their own practically. To do this required faith in God and spiritual energy, for they were to find every inch of ground contested by bitter and powerful foes. But this but gave an opportunity to prove the faithfulness of the God who had delivered them from Egypt and was now leading them on.

CHAPTER 3

"Give Me a True Token"

Joshua 2

Now therefore, I pray you, swear unto me by the LORD, since I have shown you kindness, that ye will also show kindness unto my father's house, and give me a true token. (Josh. 2:12)

By faith the harlot Rahab perished not with them that believed not, when she had received the spies with peace. (Heb. 11:31)

Likewise also was not Rahab the harlot justified by works, when she had received the messengers, and had sent them out another way? (James 2:25)

Israel's crossing the Jordan River speaks to us of our death with Christ. Joshua sent spies over to Jericho to find out the exact state of affairs, and we are told that these spies entered the city and came to a harlot's house, whose name was Rahab, and they lodged there.

A good many have questioned the immoral character of this woman Rahab and have pointed out that the word translated "harlot" does not necessarily mean an immoral woman but might simply mean a woman keeping a place of public entertainment, that is, an innkeeper; but the New Testament leaves us in no doubt as to Rahab's real character. She was like so many of her sinful sisters in that heathen land—a woman who had departed from the path of chastity and was living a wicked, unclean life. Yet God in His infinite mercy sent His messengers to this woman's house and brought deliverance not only to her own soul but to those also of her household. What a great salvation!

Christ Jesus came into the world to save sinners, not good people, not people who fancy they are good enough for God as they are, but those who are ready to take their place as lost sinners needing a Savior.

A woman went to Charles Wesley, the great hymn writer, and said to him, "Mr. Wesley, I have come to ask you to pray for me, for I am a great sinner."

Mr. Wesley answered, "Indeed, you certainly are a great sinner, and I will be glad to pray for you."

The lady exclaimed, "Who has been talking about me to you? I am just as good as anyone else in this community!"

So many people have this attitude when they go before God. God is saving sinners—those who will confess and forsake their sins.

The spies came to Rahab's house and she received them. She hid them because she knew that the authorities would soon be seeking them. In fact, it was not long until they came to her house. We read,

> The king of Jericho sent unto Rahab, saying, Bring forth the men that are come to thee, which are entered into thine house: for they be come to search out all the country. And the woman took the two men, and hid them, and said thus, There came men unto me, but I wist not whence they were: And it came to pass about the time of shutting of the gate, when it was dark, that the men went out: whither the men went I wot not: pursue after them quickly; for ye shall overtake them. (vv. 3–5)

Now Rahab did something that manifested the new attitude that she had taken toward the God of Israel. She was an idolater; she had been worshipping idols all through the years, but she had heard of the wonderful power of Jehovah, as had all her people. They had heard how God had delivered Israel out of Egypt, and of the drying up of the Red Sea, and the way He sustained this multitude throughout their journeying in the wilderness. And Rahab's soul was strangely moved. There was something about the stories which she heard that appealed to her heart, and she felt it was a divine providence that she had the representatives of the God of Israel in her house. She did what she could to protect them. She took them to the top of her house and hid them with the stalks of flax.

Rahab did not tell the truth in regard to the spies; and one might ask, "Does God commend this woman for her lying?" No, not at all, but remember her background. She had never heard the word of the law of God, "Thou shalt not bear false witness" (Exod. 20:16). She was brought up in a system that made no distinction between truth and lying. She was a poor, heathen woman who sought to know the true God by taking the wrong method in order to shield His messengers. Of course, it was wrong for her to lie, but God saw her heart, overruled the blunder she was making to protect His servants, and eventually revealed Himself to her.

"But she had brought them up to the roof of the house, and hid them with the stalks of flax, which she had laid in order upon the roof" (v. 6). In the epistle of James we are told that "Rahab the harlot [was] justified by works, when she had received the messengers, and had sent them out another way? For as the body without the spirit is dead, so faith without works is dead also" (2:25–26). When she hid the spies she showed the real faith that was in her heart. Her faith was manifested by her works in hiding them and sending them away safely. Whenever there is genuine faith in God it will always be accompanied by good works. We are not saved by works. Let no one make a mistake as to that. Scripture is absolutely clear that we are saved by grace alone through faith, and that not of ourselves; it is the gift of God. "Faith cometh by hearing, and hearing by the word of God" (Rom. 10:17). "Not of works, lest any man should boast" (Eph. 2:9). But on the other hand, where there is genuine faith, where people really believe God, where they truly receive His testimony, their faith will be manifested by their works, and that is what the apostle James stresses.

> And before they were laid down, she came up unto them upon the roof; and she said unto the men, I know that the LORD hath given you the land, and that your terror is fallen upon

us, and that all the inhabitants of the land faint because of you. (vv. 8–9)

All the people had heard about the God of Israel, and they were filled with terror, but they had no desire to know Him. In this Rahab was different from the rest. She wanted to acquaint herself with the God of Israel, and she grasped this wonderful opportunity that had come to her in order that He might be made known to her.

She continued to say,

> We have heard how the LORD dried up the water of the Red sea for you, when ye came out of Egypt; and what ye did unto the two kings of the Amorites, that were on the other side Jordan, Sihon, and Og, whom ye utterly destroyed. And as soon as we had heard these things, our hearts did melt, neither did there remain any more courage in any man, because of you: for the LORD your God, he is God in heaven above, and in earth beneath. (vv. 10–11)

A wonderful confession, "The LORD your God, he is God in heaven above, and in earth beneath"! By faith Rahab the harlot made this confession. She had committed her soul to this true and living God. We are told in Romans 10:9–10, "If thou shalt confess with thy mouth the Lord Jesus, and shalt believe in thine heart that God hath raised him from the dead, thou shalt be saved. For with the heart man believeth unto righteousness; and with the mouth confession is made unto salvation." Do not make any mistake.

There is no merit in the confession. You are not saved by *confessing* Christ; you are saved by *trusting* Christ. You confess Him because you are saved. God is calling upon all who are still in their sins to put their trust in the Lord Jesus Christ, to turn to Him and then confess Him as their Savior and Lord. He says, "Whosoever therefore shall confess me before men, him will I confess also before my Father which is in heaven" (Matt. 10:32). I am sure there are people who have trusted Christ but do not say anything about it to other folk, but I know that they are not triumphant and happy. Victorious Christians are those who delight to confess the name of Jesus. Rahab had no difficulty about confessing her faith in the one true and living God. But she wanted assurance of future security, so before these men left she said to them,

> Now therefore, I pray you, swear unto me by the LORD, since I have shown you kindness, that ye will also show kindness unto my father's house, and *give me* a *true token*. (v. 12, italics added)

Is that what your heart is saying? Are you crying, "Oh give me a true token; give me definite, positive assurance that God has really saved me"? Well, thank God, He gives such a true token in His Word. Rahab was concerned not only for herself, but for her household as well. And when people really know the Lord then they are concerned about the salvation of others—those whom they love, their own household. She continued,

> And that ye will save alive my father, and my mother, and my brethren, and my sisters, and all that they have, and deliver our lives from death. (v. 13)

In this Rahab showed a remarkable understanding of the desires of the God of Israel, for all through Scripture we see it is the purpose of God, His desire and will to save His people in families, in households. If He shows mercy to one person in a household it is an indication that He wants to save every member of that family. You remember what He said of Abraham, "Shall I hide from Abraham that thing which I do . . . ?" (Gen. 18:17). (He was speaking of the judgment of Sodom and Gomorrah.) "For I know him, that he will command his children and his household after him" (Gen. 18:19). Oh, Christian fathers and mothers, what about your attitude toward your households? Have you recognized your responsibility? Are you acting for God in the home to command your children after you? I know we live in a day of self-expression when we are taught that we should not quell the natural desires of our children, and most of us have given way to this teaching. As a result we have unconverted children in our homes, whose ways are the expression of their vile, wicked, corrupt natures. Scripture says, "Foolishness is bound in the heart of a child; but the rod of correction shall drive it far from him" (Prov. 22:15).

Mrs. William Booth, wife of the first general in the Salvation Army, who reared a large family of eight children, claimed every one of them for God before they were born. She used to say, "I refuse to bring any child into the world to be damned in hell at last." She claimed every one of her children for God. In their early days some of those children thought their mother was rather stern and hard because she would not allow them to go into the things of the world like other children, but the day came when every one of them thanked their mother for standing between them and the world, and all grew up to preach Christ and seek to bring others to Him.

A tremendous responsibility rests on parents in these matters. Too many parents say, "I will let my child go just so far in the ways of the world, and I hope eventually he will come to God," only to learn that later on he does not desire to know God at all. Your child may rebel against your correction, but he will thank you for it later on when he has come to know the Lord. Your child may look upon you as old-fashioned, but when at last he has turned to Christ for salvation then he will indeed thank you for ever having sought to lead him in the way of righteousness.

Rahab was a poor woman who had gone down into the depth of sin, but now had turned to God, and her heart cried out for the deliverance of her loved ones. So she pleaded for her household.

> The men answered her, Our life for yours, if ye utter not this our business. And it shall be, when the LORD hath given us the land, that we will deal kindly and truly with thee. (v. 14)

In the New Testament we read of the Philippian jailor who came, thinking only of himself. He cried out, "Sirs, what must I do to be saved?" (Acts 16:30). Apparently his family was gathered about him. Paul said, "Believe on the Lord Jesus Christ, and thou shalt be saved, and thy house" (Acts 16:31). That night there was great rejoicing in that house. The whole household was brought to faith in Christ and they confessed His name in baptism.

If you are the only saved member in your household, lay hold of God and in faith cry to Him for salvation for the other members of your family. Live Christ before them and look to God to bring them all to Himself. In this we may closely emulate the faith of Rahab.

Then she let them down by a cord through the window: for her house was upon the town wall, and she dwelt upon the wall.

I could not help but wonder, a few years ago, whether I was looking over Rahab's house. I went to see the ruins of the very Jericho destroyed under Joshua. That ruined city was uncovered in early 1900 and they found that the walls had fallen outward. As I looked at a ruined house I wondered if it might be that of Rahab, from the window of which she had let down the spies.

She bade them:

> Get you to the mountain, lest the pursuers meet you; and hide yourselves there three days, until the pursuers be returned: and afterward may ye go your way. And the men said unto her, We will be blameless of this thine oath which thou hast made us swear. Behold, when we come into the land, thou shalt bind this line of scarlet thread in the window which thou didst let us down by: and thou shalt bring thy father, and thy mother, and thy brethren, and all thy father's household, home unto thee. And it shall be, that whosoever shall go out of the doors of thy house into the street, his blood shall be upon his head, and we will be guiltless: and whosoever shall be with thee in the house, his blood shall be on our head, if any hand be upon him. And if thou utter this our business, then we will be quit of thine oath which thou hast made us to swear. (vv. 16–20)

What a beautiful picture of God's salvation!

They gave her a scarlet cord. I take it that it was the very cord with which they had been let down. She was to bind the scarlet cord in the window so that anyone could see it. The people of the land beholding it would not have any idea what it was for, no more perhaps than an ordinary ornament. In His Word God has given to us a scarlet line and saves all who are in the house that is thus marked off from the rest of the world.

Rahab was commanded to get her father, mother, brethren, her friends and relatives, and bring them into the house. They were all protected by the scarlet cord and they would be safe in the day when the judgment should fall upon Jericho. They were sheltered by the red cord in the window.

All who are in Christ are sheltered by His precious blood. That is the true token, for the Father looks upon that. Christ has died for me; therefore my soul is safe.

"And it shall be, that whosoever shall go out of the doors of thy house into the street, his blood shall be upon his head, and we will be guiltless: and whosoever shall be with thee in the house, his blood shall be on our head, if any hand be upon him."

In other words, they said, "Rahab, we will be your surety, and you and all in your house will be saved if protected by the scarlet cord." Christ is the surety for all who put their trust in His precious blood. But if Rahab or anyone else in the house left the protection of the scarlet cord, it was at their own risk.

Dear friends, if you refuse to trust the Lord Jesus Christ, if you refuse to find shelter beneath His precious blood, in the day when God arises to shake terribly the earth and all the things that men have trusted in go to pieces, you will be left a poor, lost, ruined soul, and your blood will be on your own head because you despised the sacrifice offered by our Lord Jesus Christ.

And she said, According unto your words, so be it. And she sent them away, and they departed: and she bound the scarlet line in the window. (v. 21)

Later when the armies of Israel began crossing the Jordan and the people of Jericho were on the wall, their hearts trembled as they saw the great army coming, and when later on the priests bearing the ark marched around Jericho, blowing their trumpets, people watched and no doubt thought it was some strange enchantment, and they were filled with terror. Rahab would look out the window and would say to herself, "Our city will never be able to stand against the God of Israel." But she could say, "There is the scarlet cord in the window and I am secure." And all who will put their trust in Christ are secure through His precious blood. Such can well afford to sing:

> Under Thy wings, my God, I rest
> Under Thy shadow safely lie;
> By Thy own strength in peace possessed,
> While dread evils pass me by.
> —Anna Laetitia Waring
> "Under Thy Wings, My God, I Rest"

It is the will of God that all who believe on the Lord Jesus Christ should have this definite assurance, knowing that they are eternally secure because of the atoning blood of the Lamb.

The truth of this runs like a scarlet line all through Scripture, from Abel's lamb slain at the gate of Eden to the Lamb on the throne in the heavenly city, where all the redeemed join in the new song of redemption by His blood. If we would sing that song in heaven let us be sure we learn it here on earth.

CHAPTER 4

CROSSING THE JORDAN

Joshua 3

And Joshua rose early in the morning; and they removed from Shittim, and came to Jordan, he and all the children of Israel, and lodged there before they passed over. And it came to pass after three days, that the officers went through the host; and they commanded the people, saying, When ye see the ark of the covenant of the LORD your God, and the priests the Levites bearing it, then ye shall remove from your place, and go after it. Yet there shall be a space between you and it, about two thousand cubits by measure: come not near unto it, that ye may know the way by which ye must go: for ye have not passed this way heretofore. And Joshua said unto the people, Sanctify yourselves: for tomorrow the LORD will do wonders among you. And Joshua spake unto the priests, saying, Take up the ark of the covenant, and pass over before the people. And they took up the ark of the covenant, and went before the people. (vv. 1–6)

The time had come for which Israel had waited so long: they were about to enter the land of promise, the inheritance which God had vouchsafed to them. Had there been the energy of faith they might have gone up into that land from Kadesh-barnea, the place of opportunity, thirty-eight years before. But because of their unbelief God had turned them back and made them wander in the wilderness until all that unbelieving generation had died. Now their children were encamped in the plains of Moab, looking toward the land, but with the river Jordan rolling between them and their promised possessions.

Jordan speaks of death, with judgment following. It is the dark river flowing down to the Dead Sea. To plunge into it would have meant the drowning of all the host of Israel. But God was about to make a dry way through that mystic river as He had done forty years before through the Red Sea. We read that Israel went down into the sea and came up out of Jordan. The two coalesce, for both speak of death. The Dead Sea says Christ's death is our death. We have died with Him. The Jordan says they who die with Him live in Him, henceforth to walk in newness of life. Thank God, our Lord Jesus Christ has died for us, and those who have put their trust in Him will never come into judgment, but are passed out of death into life. God sees us linked up with the Lord Jesus Christ in His death and resurrection.

We read in the sixth chapter of Romans, "Know ye not, that so many of us as were baptized into Jesus Christ were baptized into his death? Therefore we are buried with him by baptism into death: that like as Christ was raised up from the dead by the glory of the Father, even so we also should walk in newness of life" (6:3–4). These verses we have before us are typical of this precious truth. Israel looked over to the other side of Jordan to the land God had promised them, which typifies our present inheritance in Christ, the privileges which are enjoyed by all believers who actually enter into the truth of their union with Christ in His death and resurrection.

Canaan typifies not merely heaven after we die (as in 1 Peter 1) but the heavenly experiences which are ours to enjoy while still in our mortal bodies here on earth. It is this the apostle had in view when he exclaimed, "I am crucified with Christ: nevertheless I live; yet not I, but Christ liveth in me: and the life which I now live in the flesh I live by the faith of the Son of God, who loved me, and gave himself for me" (Gal. 2:20).

The priests bearing the ark of the covenant were to go forward first. That ark typified our Lord Jesus Christ, the meeting-place between God and man. The wood of the ark spoke of His perfect humanity; the gold, of the glory of His deity. He must go down into death first to make a dry way for His people. By dying and rising again He has "abolished death, and hath brought life and immortality to light through the gospel" (2 Tim. 1:10).

In the fourth verse of Joshua 3 we read that there was to be a space maintained between the ark and the people of about two thousand cubits, which would be approximately half a mile according to our method of computation. This was to teach due reverence for the ark of God. It had to lead the way. Alone the priests were to go down into the river and then the waters would be rolled back. Christ entered into death alone. No one could participate in the work of propitiation.

> Alone He bare the cross;
> Alone its grief sustained.
> —Joseph Swain
> "On Earth the Song Begins"

We can imagine with what interest and suppressed excitement the people watched that ark, as, borne on the shoulders of the priests, it was carried down to the river. It passed on before the people, who were to share in the safety and blessing it was to ensure, but who could do nothing themselves to stem the Jordan's flow.

God's command to the priests was, "When ye are come to the brink of the water of Jordan ye shall stand still in Jordan." What a test of faith this must have been! But it was God's word and must be acted upon. Only thus could the way be opened for Israel to go dry-shod into Canaan, and only through the death of Christ could a way be opened for us to enter into the rest that remains for the people of God.

Notice verses 11–13:

> Behold, the ark of the covenant of the Lord of all the earth passeth over before you into Jordan. Now therefore take you twelve men out of the tribes of Israel, out of every tribe a man. And it shall come to pass, as soon as the soles of the feet of the priests that bear the ark of the LORD, the Lord of all the

earth, shall rest in the waters of Jordan, that the waters of Jordan shall be cut off from the waters that come down from above; and they shall stand upon an heap.

To the natural way of thinking, this might have seemed impossible, but God had given His Word and that Word never fails. The twelve men referred to were selected for a specific purpose, of which we shall read later on.

Now notice carefully verses 14–17:

And it came to pass, when the people removed from their tents, to pass over Jordan, and the priests bearing the ark of the covenant before the people; and as they that bare the ark were come unto Jordan, and the feet of the priests that bare the ark were dipped in the brim of the water, (for Jordan over-floweth all his banks all the time of harvest,) that the waters which came down from above stood and rose up upon an heap very far from the city Adam, that is beside Zaretan: and those that came down toward the sea of the plain, even the salt sea, failed, and were cut off: and the people passed over right against Jericho. And the priests that bare the ark of the covenant of the LORD stood firm on dry ground in the midst of Jordan, and all the Israelites passed over on dry ground, until all the people were passed clean over Jordan.

The people of Israel were standing there in absolute silence, reverently looking on as the ark of the covenant went down to the river Jordan. It pictures Christ going down into the dark water of death. The moment the priests' feet rested in Jordan, the waters were dried up—the waters that had already reached the point of overflowing went down to the salt sea, and the water which came down from above rolled very far back from the city Adam.

Now, I do not know where the city Adam was. It says, "The city Adam, that is beside Zaretan." You will see that those who make the maps have indicated a city called Adam near the source of the Jordan, but they put a question mark after the name because they are not sure where the city of Adam was located. That is not important, however; but I will tell you what is important: that when our Lord Jesus Christ died on the cross the waters of judgment were rolled very far back—back to the first man, Adam. Adam's sins were taken into account when Jesus died on the cross, as well as the sins of all his race. We are told in Romans 3:23–26: "For all have sinned, and come short of the glory of God; being justified freely by his grace through the redemption that is in Christ Jesus: whom God hath set forth to be a propitiation through faith in his blood, to declare his righteousness for the remission of sins that are past, through the forbearance of God; to declare, I say, at this time his righteousness: that he might be just, and the justifier of him which believeth in Jesus."

That expression, "sins that are past," refers not to our past offences, but to the sins of those who lived before the cross. All down through the ages God had been, if I may so say, saving men on credit. The actual work of propitiation or atonement had not yet been accomplished. But in view of it, God remitted the sins of all who turned to Him in repentance and faith, and when Jesus died on the Cross all these sins were settled for, as well as those of all who at any time since would receive the Lord Jesus by faith. So now God can be just and the justifier of all who believe.

The ark remained in the bed of the Jordan "until all the people were passed clean over." So Christ in His death made complete propitiation for all men everywhere, that all may be saved, if they will. God saw all who would ever believe passing through to blessing when His blessed Son died in our stead.

As we realize our identification with Him in that death, we enter into the life of joy and high privilege which is the happy portion of all who believe.

Israel did nothing to merit this deliverance. It was God who wrought in grace on their behalf. So in the work of the Cross, all has been done that needed to be done in order that sinners might be saved. Christ is Himself the Ark and He went down into death that a way might be opened for us to enter into the blessing of redemption. It is ours to believe God and so to receive the effect of Christ's work.

CHAPTER 5

THE STONES OF WITNESS

Joshua 4

And it came to pass, when all the people were clean passed over Jordan, that the LORD spake unto Joshua, saying, Take you twelve men out of the people, out of every tribe a man, and command ye them, saying, Take you hence out of the midst of Jordan, out of the place where the priests' feet stood firm, twelve stones, and ye shall carry them over with you, and leave them in the lodging place, where ye shall lodge this night. Then Joshua called the twelve men, whom he had prepared of the children of Israel, out of every tribe a man: and Joshua said unto them, Pass over before the ark of the LORD your God into the midst of Jordan, and take you up every man of you a stone upon his shoulder, according unto the number of the tribes of the children of Israel: that this may be a sign among you, that when your children ask their fathers in time to come, saying, What mean ye by these stones? Then ye shall answer them, That the waters of Jordan were cut off before the ark of the covenant of the LORD; when it passed over Jordan, the waters of Jordan were cut off: and these stones shall be for a memorial unto the children of Israel for ever. And the children of Israel did so as Joshua commanded, and took up twelve stones out of the midst of Jordan, as the LORD spake unto Joshua, according to the number of the tribes of the children of Israel, and carried them over with them unto the place where they lodged, and laid them down there. And Joshua set up twelve stones in the midst of Jordan, in the place where the feet of the priests which bare the ark of the covenant stood: and they are there unto this day. (vv. 1–9)

It has been remarked that the Old Testament is God's picture book. It teaches by type and illustration. We are told in 1 Corinthians 10:11 that "all these things happened unto them for [our] examples: and they are written for our admonition, upon whom the ends of the [ages have] come." There are a great many people who recognize the fact that some things written in the Old Testament were typical, but they hesitate to acknowledge that this is true of all. We need to learn the lesson of these words. Some will tell you that the books of the Old Testament, the so-called historical books, are largely made up of Hebrew myths and legends, and we cannot attach any credibility to them, but the Holy Spirit says, "All these things happened." Therefore, he who believes God accepts these various experiences of

Israel as actual history. In the second place, there are certain typical lessons which we learn from them. "All these things happened unto them for types."

We have seen in the previous chapter how the ark going down into the waters of Jordan typified our Lord Jesus Christ going down into the waters of death when He could say, "Deep calleth unto deep at the noise of thy waterspouts: all thy waves and thy billows are gone over me" (Ps. 42:7). By His death on the cross He has annulled him that had the power of death, that is the Devil. Through Him the fear of death is gone, and Christians can say, "God forbid that I should glory, save in the cross of our Lord Jesus Christ, by whom the world is crucified unto me, and I unto the world" (Gal. 6:14).

The believer is identified with the Lord Jesus in His death, burial, and resurrection. This comes out very clearly, very beautifully in the present chapter. We are told that when the people were clean passed over Jordan, the Lord gave another command to Joshua. The priests bearing the ark of the covenant still stood in the riverbed, but the people had passed over, when God said to Joshua,

> Take you twelve men out of the people, out of every tribe a man, and command ye them, saying, Take you hence out of the midst of Jordan, out of the place where the priests' feet stood firm, twelve stones, and ye shall carry them over with you, and leave them in the lodging place, where ye shall lodge this night. (vv. 2–3)

The twelve stones were to be a memorial of Israel's deliverance. They were to take up these stones from the riverbed and carry them to the other side, and they were to be piled up as a monument that generations to come might look upon them and remember how God delivered His people.

> Then Joshua called the twelve men, whom he had prepared of the children of Israel, out of every tribe a man: and Joshua said unto them, Pass over before the ark of the LORD your God into the midst of Jordan, and take you up every man of you a stone upon his shoulder, according unto the number of the tribes of the children of Israel: that this may be a sign among you, that when your children ask their fathers in time to come, saying, What mean ye by these stones? Then ye shall answer them, That the waters of Jordan were cut off before the ark of the covenant of the LORD; when it passed over Jordan, the waters of Jordan were cut off: and these stones shall be for a memorial unto the children of Israel for ever. (vv. 4–7)

God wanted to preserve this as a testimony. May I say that similarly the two ordinances given to Christian people were intended by God to emphasize these truths. Take the ordinance of baptism, Christian baptism which is set forth as a memorial. "As many of you as have been baptized into Christ have put on Christ" (Gal. 3:27). "Know ye not, that so many of us as were baptized into Jesus Christ were baptized into his death?" (Rom. 6:3). When a believer is baptized he is bearing testimony to the fact that Christ has died and that he takes his place in identification with Him in His death. God sees every believer dead, buried, and risen with Christ. I hesitate to participate in baptizing anyone if he does not really understand this. Baptism is not a means of salvation; baptism can only wash away the filth of the flesh, but in baptism a person is bearing witness to his death, burial, and resurrection from the dead through Jesus Christ. The intelligent person being baptized says, "I deserve to die, but Christ died in my stead; therefore His death is my death, and I take my place now in identification with Him. I have died with Him; died to all that He died to as a man. I have died to the world, to sin in the flesh; I have died to the law; I now stand on altogether different ground before God."

The other ordinance is that of the Lord's Supper. As we gather about His table to partake of the broken bread and of the cup which represent the body and the precious blood of Christ, we remember that Christ died for us, and that He is living, and is coming again to take us to be forever with Himself. When your children ask you, "What mean ye by these ordinances?" we should be prepared to say, "Our Savior died, and we died with Him; He arose in triumph, and we have been quickened together with Him. Now we are dead to that to which He died, and are called upon to live unto God." We have this set forth in the twelve stones taken out of the midst of Jordan—our resurrection with Christ.

But there was more than that. We read in verses 9–10,

> Joshua set up twelve stones in the midst of Jordan, in the place where the feet of the priests which bare the ark of the covenant stood: and they are there unto this day. For the priests which bare the ark stood in the midst of Jordan, until every thing was finished that the LORD commanded Joshua.

How that should remind us of that word that the Savior uttered before He departed to the Father! I say "that word" for in our translation we have three words, "It is finished," but in the Greek there is only one word. What Jesus cried was *tetelestai*—"completed," "finished," "consummated"—the work of redemption was finished for all those who put their trust in Him.

The twelve stones were set up in the midst of Jordan, and when the priests, bearing the ark, came up out of the river the waters came down from above and covered up those twelve stones. The Word says, "They are there unto this day." You may take that as meaning until the book of Joshua was written, but I think we dare go even further and declare, "They are there unto *this* day." There is a lesson for us in this. We can see the infinite grace of God. Christ died for us and now we are dead to the world and all its sin.

That is what the twelve stones in the midst of the Jordan tell us. They say, "I have died with Christ; I no longer belong to the world that crucified Him; I no longer come under its judgment but under grace." That does not mean that we can be careless in our behavior. As believers we should be more careful than ever as to our conduct. That is what the apostle stresses when he says, "Sin shall not have dominion over you: for ye are not under the law, but under grace" (Rom. 6:14). Again he says, "Reckon ye also yourselves to be dead indeed unto sin, but alive unto God through Jesus Christ our Lord" (Rom. 6:11).

Those twelve stones on the other side in the land of Canaan speak of resurrection with Christ. "If ye then be risen with Christ, seek those things which are above, where Christ sitteth on the right hand of God" (Col. 3:1). May I try to make this very personal?

Have you taken your place in baptism as professedly in association with our Lord Jesus Christ in His death? Are you living it out? Let me ask you, some of you dear young people who have confessed your faith in Christ in baptism, what does that mean to you? Do you recognize the fact that God now claims you as His own? You should walk absolutely apart from the world and all its toys and idols. That is what God desires for you. When you talk to some people about coming out from the world they will say that they cannot see any harm in this thing and in that thing, and yet their own lives manifest their harmfulness. They are useless Christians; they do not count for God.

I remember a young woman whom I met when I was in Texas. She was a Christian; there was no question about that. She confessed her faith in baptism, but there was one form of worldly amusement that she enjoyed very much and that was dancing. Someone challenged her, telling her that she could not witness for Christ on a ballroom floor. She replied, "I think I am as free to witness there for Christ as anywhere else."

The person who challenged her said, "If what you say is true, I cannot tell you not to go."

One night she was dancing with a young man, and as she did so she said to herself, "I ought to witness for Christ here." So she said to her dancing partner, "I want to ask you a question."

"All right," he replied, "what is it?"

She inquired, "Do you know the Lord Jesus Christ as Savior?"

He answered, "No, do you?"

"Yes," she replied, "I do indeed."

The young man exclaimed, "Then what on earth are you doing here?" Though a mere worldling he realized that there are certain standards that Christians should seek to live up to, and this woman wasn't living up to them. She said to me, "That was the last dance I ever attended. To think I had to be rebuked like that by an unsaved young man!"

Those twelve stones in the midst of Jordan, how they ought to speak to our hearts of the grace of Christ and of what He endured for us. Have you taken your place with Him so that you can say from the heart, "God forbid that I should glory, save in the cross of our Lord Jesus Christ, by whom the world is crucified unto me, and I unto the world"?

But you say, "That means giving up so many things." Yes, but you get so much more in their place.

Those twelve stones on the other side of Jordan speak of Christ in resurrection—the blessedness, the happiness, the gladness of heart that comes to the one who is consciously identified with the risen Christ.

You will not care for the poor, trivial things of this world if your heart is taken up with Him.

> And it came to pass, when all the people were clean passed over, that the ark of the LORD passed over, and the priests, in the presence of the people. And the children of Reuben, and the children of Gad, and half the tribe of Manasseh, passed over armed before the children of Israel, as Moses spake unto them: about forty thousand prepared for war passed over before the LORD unto battle, to the plains of Jericho. On that day the LORD magnified Joshua in the sight of all Israel; and they feared him, as they feared Moses, all the days of his life. And the LORD spake unto Joshua, saying, Command the

priests that bear the ark of the testimony, that they come up out of Jordan. Joshua therefore commanded the priests, saying, Come ye up out of Jordan. (vv. 11–17)

Typically, it speaks of Christ coming up out of death in resurrection life after He had completed the work of our redemption.

And it came to pass, when the priests that bare the ark of the covenant of the LORD were come up out of the midst of Jordan, and the soles of the priests' feet were lifted up unto the dry land, that the waters of Jordan returned unto their place, and flowed over all his banks, as they did before. (v. 18)

Notice just an added word here, "And the people came up out of Jordan on the tenth day of the first month, and encamped in Gilgal" (v. 19). That was their first camping place in Canaan, and there are many precious lessons connected with Gilgal which we shall notice when we come to it in our next chapter. Those twelve stones which they took out of the Jordan were set up in Gilgal.

And he spake unto the children of Israel, saying, When your children shall ask their fathers in time to come, saying, What mean these stones? Then ye shall let your children know, saying, Israel came over this Jordan on dry land. For the LORD your God dried up the waters of Jordan from before you, until ye were passed over, as the LORD your God did to the Red sea, which he dried up from before us, until we were gone over: that all the people of the earth might know the hand of the LORD, that it is mighty: that ye might fear the LORD your God for ever. (vv. 21–24)

It is precious indeed when one enters into the reality of all this. The hymn writer has expressed it beautifully in the following verses:

> Death and judgment are behind us,
> Grace and glory are before;
> All the billows rolled o'er Jesus,
> There they spent their utmost power.
>
> Jesus died, and we died with Him,
> Buried in His grave we lay,
> One with Him in resurrection,
> Now in Him in heaven's bright day.
> —Mrs. J. A. Trench
> "Death and Judgment Are Behind Us"

CHAPTER 6

LESSONS FROM GILGAL

Joshua 5

This chapter brings before us three outstanding subjects, all of which are of great importance in connection with our taking possession of the inheritance which God has given us in Christ. These may be indicated by three suggestive terms: "Sharp Knives," "Old Corn," and "The Captain of Jehovah's Host."

The first of these topics comes before us in verses 1–9:

> And it came to pass, when all the kings of the Amorites, which were on the side of Jordan westward, and all the kings of the Canaanites, which were by the sea, heard that the LORD had dried up the waters of the Jordan from before the children of Israel, until we were passed over, that their heart melted,

neither was there spirit in them any more, because of the children of Israel. At that time the LORD said unto Joshua, Make thee sharp knives, and circumcise again the children of Israel the second time. And Joshua made him sharp knives, and circumcised the children of Israel at the hill of the fore-skins. And this is the cause why Joshua did circumcise: All the people that came out of Egypt, that were males, even all the men of war, died in the wilderness by the way, after they came out of Egypt. Now all the people that came out were circumcised: but all the people that were born in the wilderness by the way as they came forth out of Egypt, them they had not circumcised. For the children of Israel walked forty years in the wilderness, till all the people that were men of war, which came out of Egypt, were consumed, because they obeyed not the voice of the LORD: unto whom the LORD sware that he would not show them the land, which the LORD sware unto their fathers that he would give us, a land that floweth with milk and honey. And their children, whom he raised up in their stead, them Joshua circumcised: for they were uncir-cumcised, because they had not circumcised them by the way. And it came to pass, when they had done circumcising all the people, that they abode in their places in the camp, till they were whole. And the LORD said unto Joshua, This day have I rolled away the reproach of Egypt from off you. Wherefore the name of the place is called Gilgal unto this day.

Israel had crossed the Jordan. They were now encamped between the river and the city of Jericho, whose high walls loomed before them. At the command of Joshua they were to go up against not only this city, but all the cities and nations that occupied the land of Canaan. In the strength of Jehovah, as they relied upon Him, they would be able to overcome these mighty foes—foes which speak to us of those wicked spirits in heavenly places who would seek to keep us from our enjoyment of our privileges in Christ.

But before attacking the enemy God called upon His people to use sharp knives upon their own flesh. The sharp knife speaks of self-judgment. Before a believer is fit to enter into combat with his spiritual enemies he needs to use this knife of self-judgment, which is the Word of God, in living power upon his own heart and life.

The rite of circumcision of old was designed by God to mark off His people from the nations around. It was a sign of separation, and it typified death to the flesh. The ancient rite is spoken of in Ephesians 2:11, as "circumcision . . . made by hands." This, for the Christian, is no longer obligatory. It characterized Judaism and the apostle Paul points out in the epistle to the Galatians that everyone who goes back to that system, which God has now set aside, and depends upon the rite of circumcision to give him favor with God has fallen from grace; that is, he has left the high ground of salvation by grace alone and descended to the low level of attempted salvation by human merit. In place of the ancient sign, we read in Romans 2:29 of the circumcision which is of the heart; that is, the putting away from the heart of every impure and unclean lust, ambition, or tendency.

In the epistle to the Colossians, believers are said to be circumcised with the circumcision of Christ; that is, His death upon the cross is counted by God as their death, and this has put an end to their old relationship as men in the flesh doing their own will in opposition to the will of God. This is to be made practical by the use of the sharp knife of self-judgment.

In Colossians 3:5–7 we read: "Mortify therefore your members which are upon the earth; fornification, uncleanness, inordinate affection, evil concupiscence, and covetousness, which is idolatry: for which things' sake the wrath of God cometh on the children of disobedience: in the which ye also walked some time, when ye lived in them." The sins mentioned here are all such as every right-minded person recognizes as vile and abominable. The child of God is to deal unsparingly with any tendency toward these things which he finds in himself. He is to recognize himself dead indeed unto sin, but alive unto God through Christ Jesus our Lord.

But there are other sins which we are not inclined to think of as so obnoxious as those mentioned above and yet sins which are great hindrances to testimony for Christ. Of these we read in Colossians 3:8–11: "But now ye also put off all these; anger, wrath, malice, blasphemy, filthy communication out of your mouth. Lie not one to another, seeing that ye have put off the old man with his deeds; and have put on the new man, which is renewed in knowledge after the image of him that created him: where there is neither Greek nor Jew, circumcision nor uncircumcision, Barbarian, Scythian, bond nor free: but Christ is all, and in all." Many a servant of Christ has nullified his testimony by bad temper and a harsh attitude toward those who do not agree with him. This is as truly of the flesh as fornication or adultery, and against it one needs to use the sharp knife.

The reason Joshua was told to command the people of Israel to carry out the ordinance of circumcision at this time was because none of those born in the wilderness had been circumcised; therefore the reproach of Egypt was still upon them: they did not bear in their bodies the sign of separation unto God. But when His Word had been submitted to, the reproach of Egypt was rolled away. The camp where they were abiding at this time was then designated Gilgal, which means "rolling" and it speaks therefore of the place of self-judgment. They went forward afterward from this camp to battle and returned there when the conflict was over. So the soldier of Christ should ever encamp at the place of self-judgment and from there go forth in the power of the Spirit to meet his foes, returning thereto when the victory has been won; or if perchance he has met with defeat, going back to Gilgal to judge himself before God.

The second subject that comes before us is "old corn," and of this we read in Joshua 5:10–12:

> And the children of Israel encamped in Gilgal, and kept the passover on the fourteenth day of the month at even in the plains of Jericho. And they did eat of the old corn of the land on the morrow after the passover, unleavened cakes, and parched corn in the selfsame day. And the manna ceased on the morrow after they had eaten of the old corn of the land; neither had the children of Israel manna any more; but they did eat of the fruit of the land of Canaan that year.

It is most interesting to note the deep significance of three different kinds of food upon which the people of Israel fed. When they kept the Passover, which speaks of Christ's death for us upon the Cross, they ate the flesh of the lamb roast with fire. Like the priests in the sanctuary they ate "those things wherewith the atonement was made." For us this speaks of feasting our souls upon the work of our blessed Lord on Calvary. This is expressed beautifully in a well-known hymn:

> To Calvary, Lord, in spirit now
> Our weary souls repair,
> To feast upon Thy dying love
> And taste its sweetness there.
> —Sir Edward Denny
> "To Calvary, Lord, in Spirit Now"

As we meditate upon what the Lord Jesus went through for us in that hour when the judgment of God fell upon Him in order that our sins might forever be put away, we are eating in spirit of the lamb roast with fire.

As Israel journeyed through the wilderness, which speaks of this present evil world, through which God's people are now passing as strangers and pilgrims, the food that sustained them was the manna from heaven. This manna, as our blessed Lord shows us in John 6, was a type of Himself as the humbled One, who trod the path of faith in this world: our great example of devotion to the Father. He said, "Moses gave you not that bread from heaven. . . . The bread of God is he which cometh down from heaven, and giveth his life unto the world" (John 6:32–33). As we dwell upon the lowly path of our Savior through this scene, we are feeding upon the manna.

Note the place where the manna was found. Morning by morning it came from heaven to earth. It was not upon the high trees or on the mountains where the people would have to climb to obtain it; nor was it down in the deep ravines where they would have to descend and search for it. It lay all about them upon the ground, on the dew, which is a type of the Holy Spirit. The manna occupied so low a place that every Israelite, when he stepped out of his tent door in the morning, had to do one of two things: he either had to gather it or trample on it. And this is exactly the place which our Lord Jesus has taken in His infinite love and grace. We may well pause and ask ourselves the question: Are we trampling on His loving-kindness or have we received Him as our blessed, adorable Savior?

The manna then was food for the wilderness, but when the people crossed over Jordan and entered into their inheritance, which speaks of our place as associated with the risen Christ in heaven, the manna ceased, and they began to feed upon the old corn of the land. Jesus said, long years afterward: "Except a corn of wheat fall into the ground and die, it abideth alone: but if it die, it bringeth forth much fruit" (John 12:24). Christ Himself was the corn of wheat who fell into the ground in death; now He has come forth in resurrection. The old corn of the land speaks of Him as the Risen One. Therefore we who have received Him by faith are bidden to set our affections on things above, where Christ sits at the right hand of God. As we are occupied with Him in the heavenlies, we will receive new strength to enable us to appropriate and enjoy our present portion as a heavenly people.

The third topic is also of deep interest: "The Captain of Jehovah's Host." Of this we read in verses 13–15:

> And it came to pass, when Joshua was by Jericho, that he lifted
> up his eyes and looked, and, behold, there stood a man over
> against him with his sword drawn in his hand: and Joshua
> went unto him, and said unto him, Art thou for us, or for our

adversaries? And he said, Nay; but as captain of the host of the LORD am I now come. And Joshua fell on his face to the earth, and did worship, and said unto him, What saith my lord unto his servant? And the captain of the LORD's host said unto Joshua, Loose thy shoe from off thy foot; for the place whereon thou standest is holy. And Joshua did so.

Joshua had evidently gone out to reconnoiter. He was looking upon Jericho, doubtless considering what might be the best method of attacking it in order to insure the capture of that walled city; but he was to learn that it was not for him to direct the armies of Israel except as the Lord Himself gave instruction. Suddenly he saw standing before him a man with a drawn sword in his hand. Joshua, apparently without fear, immediately went over to him and asked the question: "Art thou for us, or for our adversaries?" The answer was most instructive. This stranger warrior replied, "Nay; but as captain of the host of [Jehovah] am I now come." It was the angel of the covenant appearing in human form to take command of the armies of Israel. Joshua was to be subject to his control.

Recognizing immediately the supernatural character of this visitor, Joshua fell, we are told, on his face to the earth and worshipped, inquiring, "What saith my lord unto his servant?" The answer was simple, but designed to impress Israel's great chieftain with the sanctity of the Being who addressed him, "Loose thy shoe from off thy foot; for the place whereon thou standest is holy." Instantly obeying, Joshua remained prostrate before this supernatural Captain. We are not told of anything further that passed between them, but it is evident that Joshua recognized in this theophany the blessed fact that Jehovah Himself had come to lead His people to victory.

The Captain of the Lord's host is, of course, none other than that Great Captain of our salvation: the Lord Jesus Christ Himself. The angel of the covenant of the Old Testament is the Jesus of the New Testament, God manifest in flesh. May it be ours ever to yield glad subjection to His guidance and so as we follow Him and obey His Word, we shall be assured of victory over all our foes.

> Back to Gilgal, back to Gilgal,
> Let me, O my spirit, go!
> Where the stones of death lie buried
> 'Neath the mighty Jordan's flow;
> When the manna ceased from falling
> On the resurrection day—
> Back to where the shame of Egypt
> From the host was rolled away.
>
> Back to where the stones of witness
> Silent by the river stand;
> Where was ate the feast unleaven'd,
> And the old corn of the land;
> Where Jehovah's ransomed army
> For the Canaan conquest start;
> Back to where death and resurrection
> Meet the eye and fill the heart.
>
> When, by strength of God, victorious
> Thou dost bear the spoil away,
> Back unto the camp of Gilgal
> Hasten in that joyful day!

If, defeated in the conflict,
Thou dost flee before the foe,
Back to Gilgal, O my spirit—
In thy shame and sorrow go!

Till the land shall all be conquer'd,
And the palm thy hand shall bear—
Till the tent is pitched at Shiloh,
And Jehovah worshipped there.
Camp at Gilgal, start from Gilgal,
Back to Gilgal ever come!
Anchor by the ford of Jordan
Till all Canaan is thy home.

—William Blake
"Back to Gilgal"

CHAPTER 7

The Fall of Jericho

Joshua 6

Now Jericho was straitly shut up because of the children of
Israel: none went out, and none came in. (v. 1)

The walled city of Jericho was the first obstacle that met the
people of Israel as they looked forward from the camp at Gilgal
to taking possession of the inheritance, which was theirs already by
title, that is, by Jehovah's gift, but which they had to make their
own experimentally by driving out or destroying the inhabitants of
the land, who had become so vile in the sight of the Lord that He
could no longer tolerate them. Because of their unspeakably corrupt
lives the land was about to vomit them out (see Lev. 18:25). In
Abraham's day we are told that "the iniquity of the Amorites is not

yet full" (Gen. 15:16). God therefore had waited in long-suffering mercy, but now all the nations of Canaan had sunk into such depths of depravity and the land had become so utterly defiled that it could only be cleansed by judgment.

Canaan speaks, as we have seen, not primarily of heaven itself—the eternal inheritance of the believer in Christ, for there will be no foes to contest our possession there. But it speaks of our present inheritance: that rest of heart and mind which is the abiding portion of all who take God at His word and go forward in confidence to overcome their spiritual foes. "We wrestle not against flesh and blood"—our conflict is not with men—but with wicked spirits in the heavenlies, the world rulers of this darkness—that is, with Satan and his hosts, who control the minds of those who know not God and who would seek to hinder Christians from entering into and enjoying their privileges in Christ.

There is a life of blessing and victory which is the birthright portion of each child of God, but which many of us fail to appropriate by faith and enjoy practically because of indolence and selfishness.

Jericho stood as the barrier to Israel's advance and had to be destroyed before the host of the Lord could move forward.

But how were they to subjugate this walled city when they had no battering rams or other engines of war whereby to make a breach in its defenses? The answer is given in the eleventh chapter of Hebrews: "By faith the walls of Jericho fell down, after they were compassed about seven days" (v. 30). Surely there never was another siege of so strange a character!

The Captain of the Lord's host outlined the plan of procedure, as we find it in verses 2–5:

> And the LORD said unto Joshua, See, I have given into thine
> hand Jericho, and the king thereof, and the mighty men of
> valour. And ye shall compass the city, all ye men of war, and
> go round about the city once. Thus shalt thou do six days.
> And seven priests shall bear before the ark seven trumpets of
> rams' horns: and the seventh day ye shall compass the city
> seven times, and the priests shall blow with the trumpets. And
> it shall come to pass, that when they make a long blast with
> the ram's horn, and when ye hear the sound of the trumpet,
> all the people shall shout with a great shout; and the wall of
> the city shall fall down flat, and the people shall ascend up
> every man straight before him.

The instructions were implicit. There was no room for human
schemes or approved military tactics. All was ordered of the Lord
and Joshua and Israel had but to obey.

What is the Jericho that has kept many of us from fullness of
blessing? With some it is a selfish ambition: the desire for fame or for
success in some chosen pursuit. With others it is covetousness: the
yearning to accumulate wealth and to live in opulence. With others
again it is the love of worldly pleasure: the effort to find enjoyment
in the vain things that the Christless crave. Only by faith can such
obstacles be overcome. The frowning walls of Jericho must fall
before there can be spiritual progress and enjoyment of the riches of
grace in Christ Jesus.

In obedience to the word of the Lord, Israel marched once about
the city the first day, as recorded in verses 8–11:

> And it came to pass, when Joshua had spoken unto the
> people, that the seven priests bearing the seven trumpets of

rams' horns passed on before the LORD, and blew with the trumpets: and the ark of the covenant of the LORD followed them. And the armed men went before the priests that blew with the trumpets, and the rereward came after the ark, the priests going on, and blowing with the trumpets. And Joshua had commanded the people, saying, Ye shall not shout, nor make any noise with your voice, neither shall any word proceed out of your mouth, until the day I bid you shout; then shall ye shout. So the ark of the LORD compassed the city, going about it once: and they came into the camp, and lodged in the camp.

Doubtless the people of Jericho wondered at the strange sight as the army of the Lord, led by the priests with their trumpets, and the ark of the covenant, speaking of Christ Himself, marched around the city. Little did they realize that the sounding of those trumpets was both a summons to surrender and a warning of coming judgment if they refused. Such is the message God's anointed priests are sounding out to the world today.

For six days these strange proceedings went on.

And Joshua rose early in the morning, and the priests took up the ark of the LORD. And seven priests bearing seven trumpets of rams' horns before the ark of the LORD went on continually, and blew with the trumpets: and the armed men went before them; but the rearward came after the ark of the LORD, the priests going on, and blowing with the trumpets. (vv. 12–13)

Still nothing happened. The walls stood broad and high just as before, and, no doubt, the people of Jericho congratulated themselves upon the strength of their defenses and ridiculed the folly and absurdity of Joshua and his army.

But on the seventh day the change came.

> And it came to pass on the seventh day, that they rose early about the dawning of the day, and compassed the city after the same manner seven times: only on that day they compassed the city seven times. And it came to pass at the seventh time, when the priests blew with the trumpets, Joshua said unto the people, Shout; for the LORD hath given you the city. (vv. 15–16)

As Israel obeyed the command of Joshua, the Lord acted for them. The walls of Jericho fell and the host of the Lord entered in triumph, driving all their foes before them and setting the city on fire.

Implicit instruction was given to the Israelites to keep themselves from the accursed thing when the fall of the city ensued. All that was worth preserving was to be dedicated to the Lord, even as today whatever God-given talents or wealth men have are to be consecrated to Him who gave them. No Israelite was to appropriate anything for himself. What was worthless was to be burned with fire.

> And the city shall be accursed, even it, and all that are therein, to the LORD: only Rahab the harlot shall live, she and all that are with her in the house, because she hid the messengers that we sent. And ye, in any wise keep yourselves from the accursed thing, lest ye make yourselves accursed, when ye take of the accursed thing, and make the camp of Israel a

curse, and trouble it. But all the silver, and gold, and vessels of brass and iron, are consecrated unto the LORD: they shall come into the treasury of the LORD. (vv. 17–19)

At last the long silence (save for the sounding of the trumpets) was broken.

The people shouted when the priests blew with the trumpets: and it came to pass, when the people heard the sound of the trumpet, and the people shouted with a great shout, that the wall fell down flat, so that the people went up into the city, every man straight before him, and they took the city. And they utterly destroyed all that was in the city, both man and woman, young and old, and ox, and sheep, and ass, with the edge of the sword. (vv. 20–21)

So the first great obstacle to taking possession of the land had been overcome. "This is the victory that overcometh the world, even our faith" (1 John 5:4).

But what of the promise made to Rahab, she who hid the spies because of her faith and who asked for a true token? God had not forgotten her. Neither had Joshua. Provision was made for the protection of her and all who found shelter in her house, where the scarlet cord hung in the window.

Once more our minds turn to the eleventh chapter of Hebrews, where in verse 31 we read: "By faith the harlot Rahab perished not with them that believed not, when she had received the spies with peace." Her house was upon the wall and therefore exposed to grave danger, but because of her confidence in God that part of the wall fell not when the rest was destroyed. We read in verses 22–25:

But Joshua had said unto the two men that had spied out the country, Go into the harlot's house, and bring out thence the woman, and all that she hath, as ye sware unto her. And the young men that were spies went in, and brought out Rahab, and her father, and her mother, and her brethren, and all that she had; and they brought out all her kindred, and left them without the camp of Israel. And they burnt the city with fire, and all that was therein: only the silver, and the gold, and the vessels of brass and of iron, they put into the treasury of the house of the LORD. And Joshua saved Rahab the harlot alive, and her father's household, and all that she had; and she dwelleth in Israel even unto this day; because she hid the messengers, which Joshua sent to spy out Jericho.

Thus the promise of the spies to Rahab was fulfilled and she and her father's household were preserved alive. She became an honored mother in Israel, for we learn in Matthew 1:5 that she was united in marriage to Salmon, a leader in Israel, and she became the mother of Boaz, who in turn became the husband of Ruth, the grandmother of King David. Thus Rahab, of unsavory character before she was reached by divine grace, became an ancestress, after the flesh, of our blessed Lord Jesus Christ. How wondrous are the ways of God; how great His loving-kindness!

We notice in the following verses of our chapter that Joshua put Jericho under a curse, so that in after days it would be thought of from that standpoint: "The city of the curse." This is what the world is and ever will be until the Lord Jesus Christ is recognized as King of kings and Lord of lords.

> And Joshua adjured them at that time, saying, Cursed be the
> man before the LORD, that riseth up and buildeth this city
> Jericho: he shall lay the foundation thereof in his firstborn, and
> in his youngest son shall he set up the gates of it. (v. 26)

This prophecy was fulfilled long years afterward in the days
of the ungodly King Ahab, as we are told in 1 Kings 16:34. The
destruction of Jericho was the beginning of the fulfillment of God's
Word given to Moses so long before and repeated to Joshua. It was
evident that no enemy would be able to stand before His people—
that is, Jehovah's people—so long as they put their trust in Him and
kept themselves from the accursed thing. So we are told in the last
part of the chapter that "the LORD was with Joshua; and his fame
was noised throughout all the country."

As we read and ponder over this record today we should remember
that the things that were written aforetime were written for our
learning that we might be encouraged to take the path of obedience
to the Word of the Lord, and to trust in the living God in order that
we may overcome every spiritual foe and so go up in faith to possess
that which has been given us in Christ. No power can stand against
us if we are careful to give God His rightful place in our lives and so
press with confidence to take possession of our rich inheritance.

CHAPTER 8

Sin in the Camp

Joshua 7

But the children of Israel committed a trespass in the accursed thing: for Achan, the son of Carmi, the son of Zabdi, the son of Zerah, of the tribe of Judah, took of the accursed thing: and the anger of the LORD was kindled against the children of Israel. And Joshua sent men from Jericho to Ai, which is beside Beth-aven, on the east side of Beth-el, and spake unto them, saying, Go up and view the country. And the men went up and viewed Ai. And they returned to Joshua, and said unto him, Let not all the people go up; but let about two or three thousand men go up and smite Ai; and make not all the people to labour thither; for they are but few. So there went

up thither of the people about three thousand men: and they
fled before the men of Ai. And the men of Ai smote of them
about thirty and six men: for they chased them from before
the gate even unto Shebarim, and smote them in the going
down: wherefore the hearts of the people melted, and became
as water. And Joshua rent his clothes, and fell to the earth upon
his face before the ark of the LORD until the eventide, he and
the elders of Israel, and put dust upon their heads. (vv. 1–6)

The fall of Jericho in such a miraculous way, without any real
effort on Israel's part, evidently led to overconfidence and
forgetfulness of the fact that it was God alone who had destroyed
this first barrier to their possession of the land. The next city to be
subdued was small compared to Jericho and a detachment sent out
to reconnoiter reported that it would be easily captured and that
it would be quite unnecessary for the entire host to move against
it. So about three thousand men undertook to destroy it, but were
defeated ignominiously. We are told they fled before the men of Ai
and thirty-six of them were slain. It was a great shock naturally to
Joshua and to the people as a whole, but we are told at once of the
reason for the defeat.

God had commanded Israel to take nothing for themselves of the
spoil of Jericho. The silver and the gold and metallic vessels were to
be devoted to the service of the Lord, but all else was under a curse
and was to be destroyed. One man and his family failed to obey the
word of the Lord and committed a trespass in the accursed thing.
Thus Israel had no power to stand against their foes.

There are two important lessons that we may take to our own
hearts from this incident. First, note how God looked upon the twelve

tribes of Israel as a unit. They formed one nation, and what affected one part of the nation affected all. Though strife and division came in afterward, God still speaks of the twelve tribes of Israel. To them the epistle of James is addressed and the apostle Paul speaks of the resurrection as that to which "our twelve tribes, instantly serving God day and night, hoped to come." In the Christian dispensation one of the great outstanding truths set forth in the Word is that of the entity of the body of Christ. So intimately are the members of Christ linked to one another by the Spirit that it is written: "If one member suffer, all the members suffer with it; if one member be honored all the members rejoice with it." This is very precious, but it is also exceedingly solemn. As individual members of Christ we need to realize that our attitude and behavior has an effect for good or ill upon the body as a whole. We know how true this is in the human body: often some affected hidden gland is the cause of great discomfort and misery to the entire body. When this condition is rectified the whole body is freed of its distress. And so the secret of Israel's defeat at Ai was the fact that one man and his family had disobeyed the word of the Lord and committed a trespass in the accursed thing. When the defeated soldiers of Israel came fleeing for their lives back to their brethren in the camp, the hearts of the people melted. All their hopes of a speedy defeat of their enemies seemed to be at an end and they were utterly bewildered and discouraged. Their great leader himself was shocked and perplexed at what had taken place, and we are told that "Joshua rent his clothes, and fell to the earth upon his face before the ark of the LORD until the eventide, he and the elders of Israel, and put dust upon their heads." This was the expression of utter self-abnegation and grief.

We have Joshua's prayer recorded in verses 7–9:

> And Joshua said, Alas, O Lord GOD, wherefore hast thou
> at all brought this people over Jordan, to deliver us into the
> hand of the Amorites, to destroy us? would to God we had
> been content, and dwelt on the other side Jordan! O Lord,
> what shall I say, when Israel turneth their backs before their
> enemies! For the Canaanites and all the inhabitants of the
> land shall hear of it, and shall environ us round, and cut off
> our name from the earth: and what wilt thou do unto thy
> great name?

Note the two things that troubled him: "O Lord," he exclaimed,
"what shall I say, when Israel turneth their backs before their
enemies!" The story of their defeat at Ai would spread rapidly
throughout the land and the other nations of Canaan would be
encouraged to defend their cities with renewed valor, whereas before
the fear of the Lord had fallen upon them. Then Joshua also asked:
"What wilt thou do unto thy great name?" But Jehovah can be
depended upon to defend His own name. He will not condone sin
in His own people to do this. Sin must be dealt with before God
will manifest Himself openly on their behalf.

We are told that the Lord said unto Joshua:

> Get thee up; wherefore liest thou thus upon thy face? Israel
> hath sinned, and they have also transgressed my covenant
> which I commanded them: for they have even taken of the
> accursed thing, and have also stolen, and dissembled also, and
> they have put it even among their own stuff. (vv 10–11)

This was the cause of their defeat. Prayer is always good in its place, but this was not the time for prayer. It was the time to deal in unsparing judgment with the family who had committed the sin that had weakened Israel before their foes. It was because of this sin that they had no strength to stand before their enemies, and God declared that He would not be with them any more until they destroyed the cursed thing from among them.

How often similar conditions have prevailed even in the churches of God in this dispensation of grace! Hidden sin, unconfessed, unjudged, has made the people of the Lord as weak as water when they came in conflict with their satanic foes.

In accordance with the word of the Lord all Israel was called to stand before God, and Joshua cast lots to determine the particular tribe in which the guilty party was to be found. The casting of lots was an Old Testament way of determining the mind of the Lord. We read in the book of Proverbs: "The lot is cast into the lap; but the whole disposing thereof is of the LORD" (16:33). Again and again we find this method used in determining the will of God. The last time which God seems to have recognized is that recorded in the book of Acts, when the apostles cast lots to determine whether Joseph or Matthias should be appointed as successor to Judas. After the coming of the Holy Spirit on the day of Pentecost, no such method is ever indicated in the New Testament. The believer today is able to determine the will of God as he searches the Scriptures in dependence on the Holy Spirit.

The story is told of a young curate in the Church of England who was greatly helped in his understanding of the Scriptures by frequent conversations with an uneducated cobbler, who was, nevertheless, well acquainted with the Word of God. On one occasion when a friend of his, a young theologian, was visiting him, he mentioned the remarkable knowledge of the Bible which this cobbler possessed. The young theologue, in a spirit of pride, expressed a desire to meet him, saying he felt sure he could propose some questions to him on the Scriptures which he would be quite unable to answer. Upon being introduced to him in his little shop the question was put: "Can you tell me what the Urim and Thummim were?" The cobbler replied: "I don't know exactly; I understand that the words apply to something that was on the breastplate of the high priest. I know the words mean 'Lights and Perfection' and that through the Urim and Thummim the high priest was able to discern the mind of the Lord. But I find that I can get the mind of the Lord by just changing one letter. I take this blessed Book and Usim and Thummim, and I get the mind of the Lord that way."

When the lots were cast in this particular instance, the tribe of Judah was taken; then the various families of Judah stood before the Lord; lots were cast for them and the family of the Zarhites was taken. The households of this family were then brought before God and lots were cast and the household of Zabdi was taken. His household was brought man by man before the Lord and the lot fell on Achan, the guilty person whose disobedience to the word of the Lord was responsible for Israel's defeat at Ai. Adjured by Joshua to make confession of his sin and tell what he had done, Achan answered:

> Indeed I have sinned against the LORD God of Israel, and thus and thus have I done: When I saw among the spoils a goodly

Babylonish garment, and two hundred shekels of silver, and a wedge of gold of fifty shekels weight, then I coveted them, and took them; and, behold, they are hid in the earth in the midst of my tent, and the silver under it. (vv. 20–21)

Unhappily, this confession came too late. Had Achan come to God of his own accord and acknowledged his sin and brought a proper offering, doubtless there would have been forgiveness for him. But the confession wrung from him only after the lot had indicated who the wicked one was, could not avail to shield him from judgment.

We need to remember that this event occurred in the dispensation of the law. Law knows no mercy; law is absolutely just. Therefore Achan and his family had to be destroyed because of their sin. It is very evident that the family were implicated in the evil deeds of the head of the house, because the law strictly forbade putting the children to death for the sins of the parents, but inasmuch as all were devoted to judgment, it is evident that all participated in the evil. They were brought down into the valley of Achor; that is, the valley of trouble. As they stood there before the Lord and His people,

Joshua said, Why hast thou troubled us? the LORD shall trouble thee this day. And all Israel stoned him with stones, and burned them with fire, after they had stoned them with stones. And they raised over him a great heap of stones unto this day. So the LORD turned from the fierceness of his anger. Wherefore the name of that place was called, The valley of Achor, unto this day. (vv. 25–26)

It is a sad story, but it has a serious lesson for God's people everywhere. Sin in the camp will weaken the host of the Lord and hinder blessing and victory. Sin judged and dealt with leaves God free to work in the way in which He delights.

In the book of Hosea there is a word of comfort even in connection with this sad story. The Lord tells Israel that in the latter days He is going to recover them from their wandering and restore them to Himself and He will give them "the valley of Achor for a door of hope" (Hos. 2:15). The valley of Achor speaks of the trouble that we bring upon ourselves by our own sins: retributive justice because of our departure from the Lord. But if we judge ourselves before God and turn to Him in sincerity of heart, He will give deliverance, and even the valley of Achor will become an entrance into blessing.

We need to remember that grace does not set aside government. It is still true that "whatsoever a man soweth, that shall he also reap" (Gal. 6:7), and "he that doeth wrong shall receive for the wrong which he hath done: and there is no respect of persons [with God]" (Col. 3:25). We cannot sin with impunity because we are saved by grace. But on the other hand, if we judge ourselves we shall not be judged of the Lord.

CHAPTER 9

THE FALL OF AI AND
THE PROCLAMATION OF THE LAW

Joshua 8

The present chapter readily divides into two sections. In verses 1–29 we have the account of the destruction of Ai. In verses 30–35 we read of the proclamation of the Law, with the blessings for the obedient and the curses that would fall upon the disobedient.

When God's people fail to act in accordance with His will the first time they have to face some barrier to progress, they find it far harder to overcome upon making a second effort. Had it not been for hidden sin in the camp, Israel would have overcome Ai very easily, even as they overcame Jericho when they acted in accordance with the word of the Lord. But when, after dealing with Achan and his covetous household, they prepared to make a second onslaught on the little city by whose inhabitants they had been defeated before, they found it a difficult task indeed which they had to undertake.

We read in verses 1–8:

And the LORD said unto Joshua, Fear not, neither be thou dismayed: take all the people of war with thee, and arise, go up to Ai: see, I have given into thy hand the king of Ai, and his people, and his city, and his land: and thou shalt do to Ai and her king as thou didst unto Jericho and her king: only the spoil thereof, and the cattle thereof, shall ye take for a prey unto yourselves: lay thee an ambush for the city behind it. So Joshua arose, and all the people of war, to go up against Ai: and Joshua chose out thirty thousand mighty men of valour, and sent them away by night. And he commanded them, saying, Behold, ye shall lie in wait against the city, even behind the city: go not very far from the city, but be ye all ready: and I, and all the people that are with me, will approach unto the city: and it shall come to pass, when they come out against us, as at the first, that we will flee before them, (For they will come out after us) till we have drawn them from the city; for they will say, They flee before us, as at the first: therefore we will flee before them. Then ye shall rise up from the ambush, and seize upon the city: for the LORD your God will deliver it into your hand. And it shall be, when ye have taken the city, that ye shall set the city on fire: according to the commandment of the LORD shall ye do. See, I have commanded you.

Thus did God outline the plan they were to carry out; a plan intended to impress upon them the folly of underrating the power of the enemy as they had done before, and also the lesson of their own helplessness and insufficiency apart from the divine enabling.

Acting on the instruction given, we are told that

> Joshua rose up early in the morning, and numbered the people, and went up, he and the elders of Israel, before the people to Ai. And all the people, even the people of war that were with him, went up, and drew nigh, and came before the city, and pitched on the north side of Ai: now there was a valley between them and Ai. And he took about five thousand men, and set them to lie in ambush between Beth-el and Ai, on the west side of the city. And when they had set the people, even all the host that was on the north of the city, and their liers in wait on the west of the city, Joshua went that night into the midst of the valley. (vv. 10–13)

Thus all was in readiness for the test of the morrow, when the men of Ai were to learn that, after all, they were no match for Israel so long as they acted in accordance with the word of God.

Ai was a little city, and it is the little things that become great obstacles in the onward march of the host of the Lord, unless they are dealt with in the light of His Word. In this instance, Israel was to learn how strong a little city may be and what wisdom and dependence on God is needed in order to overcome it.

As anticipated and foreseen by Joshua, acting under divine direction, the men of Ai came rushing forth early in the morning expecting an easy victory, and at first it seemed as though they were right. We read:

And it came to pass, when the king of Ai saw it, that they hasted and rose up early, and the men of the city went out against Israel to battle, he and all his people, at a time appointed, before the plain; but he wist not that there were liers in ambush against him behind the city. And Joshua and all Israel made as if they were beaten before them, and fled by the way of the wilderness. And all the people that were in Ai were called together to pursue after them: and they pursued after Joshua, and were drawn away from the city. And there was not a man left in Ai or Beth-el, that went not out after Israel: and they left the city open, and pursued after Israel. (vv. 14–17)

Recklessly the self-confident men of Ai left their city utterly unprotected as they pursued after the retreating Israelites. At Joshua's signal the three thousand men in ambush then rose up and carried out the orders given on the night before:

And the LORD said unto Joshua, Stretch out the spear that is in thy hand toward Ai; for I will give it into thine hand. And Joshua stretched out the spear that he had in his hand toward the city. And the ambush arose quickly out of their place, and they ran as soon as he had stretched out his hand: and they entered into the city, and took it, and hasted and set the city on fire. (vv. 18–19)

This ruse resulted in the capture of Ai and the destruction of its inhabitants, as we read in verses 20–23:

And when the men of Ai looked behind them, they saw, and, behold, the smoke of the city ascended up to heaven, and they had no power to flee this way or that way: and the people that fled to the wilderness turned back upon the pursuers. And when Joshua and all Israel saw that the ambush had taken the city, and that the smoke of the city ascended, then they turned again, and slew the men of Ai. And the other issued out of the city against them; so they were in the midst of Israel, some on this side, and some on that side: and they smote them, so that they let none of them remain or escape. And the king of Ai they took alive, and brought him to Joshua.

It was a signal victory for Israel, though achieved in a manner designed to impress upon them the folly of acting in accordance with their own thoughts and failing to discern the mind of the Lord. They were strong only as they acted in obedience to His commands.

Details of the close of the battle are given in verses 24–29:

And it came to pass, when Israel had made an end of slaying all the inhabitants of Ai in the field, in the wilderness wherein they chased them, and when they were all fallen on the edge of the sword, until they were consumed, that all the Israelites returned unto Ai, and smote it with the edge of the sword. And so it was, that all that fell that day, both of men and women, were twelve thousand, even all the men of Ai. For Joshua drew not his hand back, wherewith he stretched out the spear, until he had utterly destroyed all the inhabitants of Ai. Only the cattle and the spoil of that city Israel took for a prey unto themselves, according unto the word of the LORD which he commanded Joshua. And Joshua burnt Ai, and made it an heap for ever, even a desolation unto this day. And the king of Ai he hanged on a tree until eventide: and as soon as the sun was down, Joshua commanded that they should take his carcase down from the tree, and cast it at the entering of the gate of the city, and raise thereon a great heap of stones, that remaineth unto this day.

Observe that in this instance God permitted Israel to take the cattle and the wealth of the city as a prey for themselves. He did not put a ban on the spoil of Ai as on that of Jericho. There are certain things of an earthly character which God's children are permitted to use for sustenance and enjoyment, even though they are called upon to judge the world as an ordered system opposed to the cross of Christ.

We turn now to the second section. Moses had commanded the children of Israel that when they entered into the land they were to proceed to the Mounts Gerizim and Ebal and there set up an altar and a pillar and proclaim the law, with its statutes and judgments, as given first at Sinai and amplified in the plains of Moab. Of this we read in Deuteronomy 27 and 28.

In accordance with this command, we are told in Joshua that

Joshua built an altar unto the LORD God of Israel in mount Ebal, as Moses the servant of the LORD commanded the children of Israel, as it is written in the book of the law of Moses, an altar of whole stones, over which no man hath lift up any iron: and they offered thereon burnt-offerings unto the LORD, and sacrificed peace offerings. (vv. 30–31)

This altar, observe, was built of whole stones, upon which no tool had been lifted, as Moses had told them in Exodus 20:25. The altar speaks of Christ, as does the offering placed upon it. He had to be who He was in order to do what He did. Therefore, there was to be no effort by man to shape the stones. They were to be put together just as they were provided by God. Upon this altar burnt offerings and peace offerings were placed. These speak of Christ offering Himself without spot unto God on our behalf and thus making peace by the blood of His cross.

It was most blessed that such a foreshadowing was seen at the base of Mount Ebal—for from that mount the curses were declared by one half of the Levites. All are under the curse to whom the law comes, for "cursed is every one that continueth not in all things which are written in the book of the law to do them" (Gal. 3:10). That smoking altar told of Him who, sinless Himself, was to make propitiation for the sins of the world.

The blessings were proclaimed by the other half of the Levites from Mount Gerizim (Deut. 27:12), but as these blessings depended entirely upon the obedience of the people, it was soon manifest that no man could claim them as being rightfully his. All blessing must be on the ground of pure grace.

After the sacrifices were offered, the altar was, as it were, turned into a monument. It was covered with plaster, on which, when hardened, the blessings and the curses were written as a memorial "according to all that is written in the book of the law" (Josh. 8:34). This was to be an abiding testimonial that it might not be forgotten in days to come:

> There was not a word of all that Moses commanded, which Joshua read not before all the congregation of Israel, with the women, and the little ones, and the strangers that were conversant among them. (v. 35)

Thus had Joshua begun to take possession of the land which by this monument was dedicated to Jehovah. But because of Israel's disobedience, the time came when God could no longer own them as His covenant people and so He gave them over to the power of their enemies. It is not possible for fallen man to keep God's perfect law. That law which in itself is "holy, just, and good," can only curse and condemn those who are under it. In the fullness of time Christ came to redeem from that curse all who believe in Him. Now His redeemed people stand before God on the ground of pure grace, and their obedience, far from being of a legal character, is the glad service of love to Him who has made them His own.

CHAPTER 10

THE WILES OF THE DEVIL

Joshua 9

It has been well said that "Satan plays with loaded dice." He knows all the weaknesses of human nature and is an expert in the black art of deception. So in the New Testament believers are exhorted to "put on the whole armour of God, that [they] may be able to stand against the wiles of the devil" (Eph. 6:11).

We have a very striking illustration of the Devil's deceptive practices in this ninth chapter of Joshua. As the word went out to the other Canaanite peoples that Jericho and Ai had fallen before the victorious Israelites, the dwellers in a certain Hivite city, named Gibeon, decided that if they would avert the destruction of themselves and their city, they must act at once and that in a manner calculated to mislead Joshua and his forces regarding their identity and the location of their homeland.

So we are told in verses 3–6:

> And when the inhabitants of Gibeon heard what Joshua had done unto Jericho and to Ai, they did work wilily, and went and made as if they had been ambassadors, and took old sacks upon their asses, and wine bottles, old, and rent, and bound up; and old shoes and clouted upon their feet, and old garments upon them; and all the bread of their provision was dry and mouldy. And they went to Joshua unto the camp at Gilgal, and said unto him, and to the men of Israel, We be come from a far country: now therefore make ye a league with us.

This was on the part of these Hivites a very clever ruse and it accomplished its purpose, for when the strange-looking "ambassadors" arrived at the camp of Israel in Gilgal, Joshua and his officers were deceived by their appearance and the story that they concocted. The ragged garments, the worn-out sandals, the rotting wineskins, and the moldy bread all seemed to authenticate the plea that these Gibeonites made.

> And the men of Israel said unto the Hivites, Peradventure ye dwell among us; and how shall we make a league with you? And they said unto Joshua, We are thy servants. And Joshua said unto them, Who are ye? and from whence come ye? And they said unto him, From a very far country thy servants are come because of the name of the LORD thy God: for we have heard the fame of him, and all that he did in Egypt, and all that he did to the two kings of the Amorites, that were beyond

Jordan, to Sihon king of Heshbon, and to Og king of Bashan, which was at Ashtaroth. Wherefore our elders and all the inhabitants of our country spake to us, saying, Take victuals with you for the journey, and go to meet them, and say unto them, We are your servants: therefore now make ye a league with us. This our bread we took hot for our provision out of our houses on the day we came forth to go unto you; but now, behold, it is dry, and it is mouldy: and these bottles of wine, which we filled, were new; and, behold, they be rent: and these our garments and our shoes are become old by reason of the very long journey. (vv. 7–13)

There was something so apparently genuine about this recital, with its hypocritical pretense of having come to fear Jehovah, the God of Israel, that those who listened to it were quite carried away by it. We are told, "the men took of their victuals, and asked not counsel . . . of the LORD" (v. 14). This was a fatal mistake. It is always wrong to act on our own judgment instead of seeking to know the mind of God as revealed in His Word.

Had Joshua and the rest remembered the instruction given them to destroy utterly the corrupt nations of Canaan, they would have been careful to make further inquiry before accepting the story of the men of Gibeon at face value. But, as we so often are inclined to do, they trusted their own judgment and so were misled completely. Verse 15 tells us:

And Joshua made peace with them, and made a league with them, to let them live: and the princes of the congregation sware unto them.

How the wily Gibeonites must have laughed in their sleeves as they noted the success of their scheme! Joshua had failed to discern their hypocrisy. When he and the princes of the congregation had made a league with these deceivers, the latter departed in high glee, to inform their fellow citizens that they were now allies of Israel and so the danger of their extirpation had passed!

May we not see in this how Satan works today? Knowing he cannot by any means affect the eternal destiny of the people of God, he uses all kinds of schemes to mislead them here on earth and to turn them aside from full obedience to the will of God. He never comes to a Christian presenting himself in his true character. He appears as an angel of light with suggestions which appeal to the natural mind, just as he came to Eve of old, who was deceived by his wiles and thus the old creation went down with a crash.

Whatever plan he suggests will be seen in its true light if tested by what God has revealed in His Word: "To the law and to the testimony: if they speak not according to this word, it is because there is no light in them" (Isa. 8:20). Yet those who should know better are often led astray by specious suggestions and flattering words and so enter into associations and are led to pursue plans which work havoc to their own spirituality and make them useless to others who need their help.

Perhaps there is nothing whereby Satan has lured more young Christians into paths of disobedience and lifetime wretchedness than by the snare of mixed marriages. God has plainly forbidden the unequal yoke (see 2 Cor. 6:14). Yet when Satan manages to get the affections engaged and the hearts of two are drawn together—the one a Christian and the other an unbeliever—it is easy to allow one's personal desires to overrule God's plain testimony. In the hope that after all He will be better than His Word, the child of God enters into a union entailing lifelong misery. The same is true as to many other relationships: business partnerships with the ungodly, joining lodges and other societies that link saved and unsaved together, and, most insidious of all, the union of children of God and children of the Devil in church fellowship!

Israel soon discovered the mistake they had made, but it was then too late to extricate themselves from the mess into which they had fallen (vv. 16–18):

> And it came to pass at the end of three days after they had made a league with them, that they heard that they were their neighbours, and that they dwelt among them. And the children of Israel journeyed, and came unto their cities on the third day. Now their cities were Gibeon, and Chephirah, and Beeroth, and Kirjath-jearim. And the children of Israel smote them not, because the princes of the congregation had sworn unto them by the LORD God of Israel. And all the congregation murmured against the princes.

In an effort to alleviate the condition to some extent, it was determined that the spared Gibeonites should become servants to the Israelites, as we read in verses 19–21:

> But all the princes said unto all the congregation, We have sworn unto them by the LORD God of Israel: now therefore we may not touch them. This we will do to them; we will even let them live, lest wrath be upon us, because of the oath

which we sware unto them. And the princes said unto them,
Let them live; but let them be hewers of wood and drawers of
water unto all the congregation; as the princes had promised
them.

This was the best they could do under the circumstances which
they had brought upon themselves, and many a believer since has
sought in a similar way to bend the results of his folly to his own
service, only to find that it has entailed conditions which have been
perplexing and bewildering through all the years ahead.

Joshua was the spokesman for the princes. He said to the
Gibeonites:

Wherefore have ye beguiled us, saying, We are very far from
you; when ye dwell among us? Now therefore ye are cursed,
and there shall none of you be freed from being bondmen,
and hewers of wood and drawers of water for the house of my
God. (vv. 22–23)

Glad to have saved their lives at any cost, the Hivites accepted the
situation as gracefully as they could.

And they answered Joshua, and said, Because it was certainly
told thy servants, how that the LORD thy God commanded his
servant Moses to give you all the land, and to destroy all the
inhabitants of the land from before you, therefore we were sore
afraid of our lives because of you, and have done this thing.
And now, behold, we are in thine hand: as it seemeth good
and right unto thee to do unto us, do. (vv. 24–25)

In this way, the matter was closed for the time, as we read in verses 26–27:

> And so did he unto them, and delivered them out of the hand of the children of Israel, that they slew them not. And Joshua made them that day hewers of wood and drawers of water for the congregation, and for the altar of the LORD, even unto this day, in the place which he should choose.

How much better it would have been, both for Israel and for Gibeon, if these Canaanites had come to Joshua in all honesty and made peace with Israel by accepting the amnesty which was offered freely to all who acknowledged the claims of Jehovah, the one true and living God, even as we are told in Deuteronomy 20:10–12: "When thou comest nigh unto a city to fight against it, then proclaim peace unto it. And it shall be, if it make thee answer of peace, and open unto thee, then it shall be, that all the people that is found therein shall be tributaries unto thee, and they shall serve thee. And if it will make no peace with thee, but will make war against thee, then thou shalt besiege it."

According to this Word of the Lord, had the men of Gibeon and the adjoining cities come to Joshua and frankly acknowledged the power and authority of Jehovah, seeking to make peace with Israel by complete surrender, their cities would have been spared, their lives saved, and an honorable league would have been entered into. But they chose instead to take the path of deception, which led to bondage and servitude.

Today God has commissioned His servants to go to all men everywhere, "preaching peace by Jesus Christ" (Acts 10:36). All who receive the message in faith, who bow in repentance at the feet of the risen Savior are justified by faith and have peace with God. For Christ has made peace by the blood of His cross. Those thus saved are united to the church of the living God and become in turn His messengers to carry the gospel to others.

There is no occasion for deception or hypocrisy, which can only result in greater disaster, for "the hypocrite's hope shall perish." But when there is frank confession of sin, God stands ready in faithfulness and justice to forgive all sin and to cleanse from all unrighteousness. None can be too vile for Christ. None need fear to come to Him for salvation, for He has said, "Him that cometh to me I will in no wise cast out." Blessed are they who take Him at His Word and trust His grace!

CHAPTER 11

WHEN THE SUN STOOD STILL

Joshua 10

The evil effects of the unhappy alliance with the men of Gibeon soon began to be manifested. When the nations of the contiguous territories learned what had taken place, they formed a confederation, headed by Adonizedek, king of Jerusalem, and set out to attack Gibeon, as a warning to the people of other districts, not to make peace with Israel. This at once led the Gibeonites to call for help from their new allies, and in order to redeem their pledges it became necessary for Joshua to lead the host of the Lord up from Gilgal to attack the confederated armies. Had it not been for the blunder into which they had been betrayed by failing to consult the Lord, they would not have had to meet so vast an army at one time, but the conquest of Canaan would have proceeded in a more orderly way as city after city should have fallen before them, even as Jericho and Ai had done.

We have seen that the seven nations of Canaan, who were determined to contest Israel's right to take possession of the land, picture for us the spiritual foes who ever seek to hinder our entering into the enjoyment of the inheritance which is ours by title from the moment we are saved. We wrestle not with flesh and blood but with wicked spirits in the heavenlies, the world rulers of this darkness, or, the rulers of this dark world. Of these Satan is the chief, even as Adonizedek headed up the coalition against Israel.

We know that a former king of Jerusalem, Melchizedek, was priest of the Most High God and was a type of our resurrected Lord, made a high priest forever after the order of Melchizedek, a name that means "King of Righteousness." Adonizedek means "lord of righteousness." He was not a priest of the Most High, but was the avowed enemy of the people of God. In this he pictures Satan, the accuser of the brethren, who accuses them before our God day and night. Pretending to be concerned about the maintaining of righteousness on the part of those who profess faith in Christ, he both seeks to lead them into sin and then accuses them of unrighteousness when or if they yield to the temptations he sets before them. Thus he seems to be the lord of righteousness, and his ministers, we are told, pass for ministers of righteousness (see 2 Cor. 11:13–15). In meeting such, we need to remember that "(the weapons of our warfare are not carnal, but mighty through God to the pulling down of strong holds;) casting down imaginations, and every high thing that exalteth itself against the knowledge of God, and bringing into captivity every thought to the obedience of Christ" (2 Cor. 10:4–5).

It is of this conflict in the heavenlies that the opening verses of our chapter speak if we look at them in their typical aspect.

> Now it came to pass, when Adoni-zedek king of Jerusalem had heard how Joshua had taken Ai, and had utterly destroyed it; as he had done to Jericho and her king, so he had done to Ai and her king; and how the inhabitants of Gibeon had made peace with Israel, and were among them; that they feared greatly, because Gibeon was a great city, as one of the royal cities, and because it was greater than Ai, and all the men thereof were mighty. Wherefore Adoni-zedek king of Jerusalem sent unto Hoham king of Hebron, and unto Piram king of Jarmuth, and unto Japhia king of Lachish, and unto Debir king of Eglon, saying, Come up unto me, and help me, that we may smite Gibeon: for it hath made peace with Joshua and with the children of Israel. Therefore the five kings of the Amorites, the king of Jerusalem, the king of Hebron, the king of Jarmuth, the king of Lachish, the king of Eglon, gathered themselves together, and went up, they and all their hosts, and encamped before Gibeon, and made war against it. (Josh. 10:1–5)

In their terror and alarm, the Gibeonites appealed to Joshua for help.

> And the men of Gibeon sent unto Joshua to the camp of Gilgal, saying, Slack not thy hand from thy servants; come up to us quickly, and save us, and help us: for all the kings of the Amorites that dwell in the mountains are gathered together against us. So Joshua ascended from Gilgal, he, and

all the people of war with him, and all the mighty men of valour. (vv. 6–7)

Although this conflict was precipitated by their own failure, yet God in His grace gave assurance to His servants that He would destroy their foes as they went up against them in dependence on His might:

And the LORD said unto Joshua, Fear them not: for I have delivered them into thine hand; there shall not a man of them stand before thee. (v. 8)

Acting in accordance with the word of the Lord, Joshua came upon the allied Canaanite armies suddenly, going up from Gilgal all night. He attacked the detachments besieging Gibeon first, and defeated them utterly. As they fled with Israel pursuing, panic overtook the other Canaanites and they did not even attempt a united stand against the host of the Lord.

The battle raged all day long, and as twilight was falling the event occurred at which skeptics have sneered for all the centuries since.

Then spake Joshua to the LORD in the day when the LORD delivered up the Amorites before the children of Israel, and he said in the sight of Israel, Sun, stand thou still upon Gibeon; and thou, Moon, in the valley of Ajalon. And the sun stood still, and the moon stayed, until the people had avenged themselves upon their enemies. Is not this written in the book of Jasher? So the sun stood still in the midst of heaven, and hasted not to go down about a whole day. And there was no day like that before it or after it, that the LORD hearkened unto the voice of a man: for the LORD fought for Israel. (vv. 12–14)

Just what did take place we may not know; whether an actual day was lost in astronomical reckoning, as some reputable scientists have insisted, or whether by the phrase, "the sun stood still," we are to understand a miracle of refraction, we cannot say, but we do know from the inspired record that the light continued for nearly another whole day, until all the battered hosts of the allies were destroyed and their kings taken captive. Scripture uses the language to which men are accustomed. We speak of the sun rising and setting, even though we understand that this is not literally true. So with the expression "the sun stood still." To human sight this was a fact. How it came to pass we can leave with God.

Following this great victory, Joshua returned to Gilgal, the place of self-judgment. There the five confederate kings were brought out from the caves in which they had been imprisoned while the battle went on and we are told that:

When they brought out those kings unto Joshua, that Joshua called for all the men of Israel, and said unto the captains of the men of war which went with him, Come near, put your feet upon the necks of these kings. And they came near, and put their feet upon the necks of them. (v. 24)

How this reminds us of Romans 16:20: "The God of peace shall bruise Satan under your feet shortly."

This great victory was followed by attacks upon city after city and the discomfiture and utter destruction of their defenders. After each new victory the triumphant Israelites returned to Gilgal, there to give thanks to God, who had thus given deliverance, as He had promised.

The series of victories is summed up for us in verses 40–43:

> So Joshua smote all the country of the hills, and of the south, and of the vale, and of the springs, and all their kings: he left none remaining, but utterly destroyed all that breathed, as the LORD God of Israel commanded. And Joshua smote them from Kadesh-barnea even unto Gaza, and all the country of Goshen, even unto Gibeon. And all these kings and their land did Joshua take at one time, because the LORD God of Israel fought for Israel. And Joshua returned, and all Israel with him, unto the camp to Gilgal.

Thus had God fulfilled His Word, for "He is faithful that promised." The judgment of the Canaanites long deferred until the patience of God came to an end was the manifestation of His holy detestation of the abominable idolatrous rites and the vile immoral habits that characterized these nations. The description of the heathen world given in Romans 1 will give the reader some idea of the filthy behavior of these people. They had defiled the land by their lasciviousness and God commanded their destruction accordingly.

Thus the way was opened for Israel to take full possession of the inheritance which God had given them although there were yet other enemies to be destroyed.

CHAPTER 12

GOD'S WORD TESTED AND PROVEN

Joshua 11–12

Admittedly these chapters and most of those to follow do not lend themselves readily to expository preaching. Yet we would not forget that "all Scripture is God-breathed and profitable"; so we may be sure that these portions were written for our admonition and have in them precious lessons we cannot afford to pass over lightly.

In the opening verses of chapter 11 we read of the second, and, as it turned out, the last great coalition of Canaanite nations that Joshua and the Lord's host had to face before they could take possession of their promised inheritance. This time it was a confederation headed by Jabin, king of Hazor, and with him were associated Jobab, king of Madon, and the kings or sheiks who held authority over the tribes on the north of the mountains of Palestine and in the great plains south of Chinneroth, that is, the sea of Galilee. The Canaanites who dwelt in the east and on the west, and the remnants of the Amorites, Hittites, Perizzites, Jebusites, and Hivites also sent their quotas. It was a formidable host indeed, but Joshua went out to meet them strong in the Lord and in the power of His might; and the result is given us in 11:6–9:

> And the LORD said unto Joshua, Be not afraid because of them: for tomorrow about this time will I deliver them up all slain before Israel: thou shalt hough their horses, and burn their chariots with fire. So Joshua came, and all the people of war with him, against them by the waters of Merom suddenly; and they fell upon them. And the LORD delivered them into the hand of Israel, who smote them, and chased them unto great Zidon, and unto Misrephoth-maim, and unto the valley of Mizpeh eastward; and they smote them, until they left them none remaining. And Joshua did unto them as the LORD bade him: he houghed their horses, and burnt their chariots with fire.

Hazor was the metropolis of that entire section, it would seem, and having defeated its king and his allies, we read that:

> Joshua at that time turned back, and took Hazor, and smote the king thereof with the sword: for Hazor beforetime was the head of all those kingdoms. And they smote all the souls that were therein with the edge of the sword, utterly destroying them: there was not any left to breathe: and he burnt Hazor with fire. (11:10–11)

As intimated before, it is only as we realize something of the unspeakably vile character of these wretched people that we can understand why God ordered their utter extermination. He had borne with them until the cup of their iniquity was full to overflowing; then, in His righteousness as the Moral Governor of the universe, He decreed their destruction. Joshua was His instrument in carrying out this judgment and he did his work faithfully, as we are told in verses 15–20. God's love had given the Canaanites many years in which to repent, had there been on their part any desire to be delivered from their manifold iniquities. Instead of that they had sunk deeper and deeper into the pit of corruption and vileness until there was no remedy. The very mercy of God had but hardened them in their sins; so judgment had to be meted out according to their works.

Some of the ancient inhabitants of the land, the Anakim, a race of men of giant stature who had been driven back into the mountains by those who came in later, were also destroyed, except for a small remnant who dwelt in the Philistine cities, some of whom were slain by David and his associates in after years.

We read in 11:23:

> So Joshua took the whole land, according to all that the LORD said unto Moses; and Joshua gave it for an inheritance unto Israel according to their divisions by their tribes. And the land rested from war.

Thus God's word had been tested and proven. He had kept every promise He made when He first commissioned Joshua to go over the Jordan and take possession of the land; He had assured him that

He would destroy the enemies before Israel and that if they kept His law and acted in accordance with His commands they would never know defeat! And so it had come to pass.

The twelfth chapter gives us a list of the many kings who had fallen before Israel's triumphant march, from the day that they met the Amorites and the king of Bashan on the eastern side of the Jordan and of the lake of Chinneroth until the last of the cities of Canaan had submitted to them. The lands of Sihon and of Og had been allotted already to the tribes of Reuben and Gad and the half tribe of Manasseh. The territories of the kings on the west of the Jordan were now to be divided among the other nine and a half tribes. Of this the following chapters treat in detail.

Joshua's victories illustrate the Christian's triumph over the unseen hosts of evil who, acting under the leadership of Satan, the god and prince of this world, would seek to hinder believers from possessing practically that which God has given them in Christ Jesus.

Many of us are defeated, when we ought to be victors, because of unjudged sin in our lives, or because of sloth and lethargy which hinder our laying hold of that for which God has laid hold of us. Blessed it is, if, like the apostle Paul, we recognize the importance of "pressing on toward the mark for the prize of the calling of God on high in Christ Jesus" (Phil. 3:14, literal rendering). When God has promised to lead us on from victory to victory if we but cleave to Him with purpose of heart, it is the greatest folly to hold back and to fear lest we may not be able to overcome in the day of adversity. We may well take to heart the admonition of Philippians 3:15–16: "Let us therefore, as many as be perfect, be thus minded: and if in any thing ye be otherwise minded, God shall reveal even this unto you. Nevertheless, whereto we have already attained, let us walk by the same rule, let us mind the same thing." Let us hold fast what God has revealed to us already and go forward in dependence upon His Holy Spirit to appropriate the precious things into which we have not yet entered. We often sing contentedly:

> There are depths of love that I cannot know
> Till I cross the narrow sea;
> There are heights of joy that I may not reach
> Till I rest in peace with Thee.
>
> —Fanny Crosby
> "I Am Thine, O Lord"

While this is true, and there will ever be more to enter into and enjoy than we can possibly know on earth, yet we should not settle down contented to make no further progress because God has led us on into the enjoyment of some measure of His truth.

A dear brother used often to suggest that this verse be changed so that we should sing:

> There are depths of love that I yet may know
> Ere I cross the narrow sea;
> There are heights of joy that I yet may reach
> Ere I rest in peace with Thee.

This is surely true. We should ever be moving on from one victory to another, proving anew from day to day the faithfulness of our gracious God and the trustworthiness of His promises!

CHAPTER 13

CALEB, THE WHOLEHEARTED, ON THE ENERGY OF FAITH

Joshua 13–14

The wars of Canaan were largely at an end. Israel had to a great extent found at least temporary rest in the land that God had promised them. We know from the history that follows that this condition, however, did not continue. In the epistle to the Hebrews we are told, "If Jesus had given them rest, He would not have spoken of another rest" (4:8, author's translation). Many, perhaps, have not realized that *Jesus* and *Joshua* are the same: that is, Joshua is the Hebrew form of the name that our blessed Lord bore here on earth. *Jesus* is an Anglicization of the Greek form. So the passage in Hebrews is referring to the rest into which Joshua led the people, which did not prove to be lasting because of the faithlessness of Israel, and yet in the beginning of their history there was certainly much to give them confidence as they saw how marvelously God undertook for them.

As the thirteenth chapter opens we hear the Lord addressing Joshua, now an aged man. God said to him:

> Thou art old and stricken in years, and there remaineth yet very much land to be possessed. (13:1)

Then in the rest of the chapter we have pointed out vast tracks of the land not yet settled by Israel, even though they had to a very large extent overcome their enemies and taken possession of many of their cities and villages.

We learn too of the judgment meted out to Balaam, who sought to destroy Israel by giving evil advice to Balak. In 13:22 it tells us also,

> Balaam . . . did the children of Israel slay with the sword among them that were slain by them.

Several of the tribes had already obtained their inheritance, but the others had not yet taken possession of the land that was to be allotted to them; and so the challenge was given: "There remaineth yet very much land to be possessed."

Surely these words may speak loudly to our hearts. Many of us have known the Lord for years. To what extent have we really entered into the enjoyment of the precious things of Christ which are ours by title? Have we not been content to know that our souls are saved and that we shall spend eternity in heaven, while failing to enter into the reality and blessedness of a "life hid with Christ in God" as we pass through this scene? Then, too, think of the great treasure committed to us in the Word of God. Those of us who have given the most time to careful study and meditation over God's blessed Book must realize that still "there remaineth yet very much land to be possessed." Large portions of Scripture are still to most of us a kind of a literary *terre incognita*. We are familiar, perhaps, with the great outstanding truths of Scripture, and certain precious chapters have ever been our joy and delight, but there is so much more in the Scriptures that we need to make our own by careful study in dependence on the Holy Spirit of God. In the energy of faith we are called upon to take possession of that which is already ours through the gift of God. In the story of Caleb we see this energy of faith blessedly illustrated. We read in chapter 14, beginning with verse 6 through verse 15:

> Then the children of Judah came unto Joshua in Gilgal: and Caleb the son of Jephunneh the Kenezite said unto him, Thou knowest the thing that the LORD said unto Moses the man of God concerning me and thee in Kadesh-barnea. Forty years old was I when Moses the servant of the LORD sent me from Kadesh-barnea to espy out the land; and I brought him word again as it was in mine heart. Nevertheless my brethren that went up with me made the heart of the people melt: but I wholly followed the LORD my God. And Moses sware on that day, saying, Surely the land whereon thy feet have trodden shall be thine inheritance, and thy children's for ever, because thou hast wholly followed the LORD my God. And now, behold, the LORD hath kept me alive, as he said,

these forty and five years, even since the LORD spake this word unto Moses, while the children of Israel wandered in the wilderness: and now, lo, I am this day fourscore and five years old. As yet I am as strong this day as I was in the day that Moses sent me: as my strength was then, even so is my strength now, for war, both to go out, and to come in. Now therefore give me this mountain, whereof the LORD spake in that day; for thou heardest in that day how the Anakims were there, and that the cities were great and fenced: if so be the LORD will be with me, then I shall be able to drive them out, as the LORD said. And Joshua blessed him, and gave unto Caleb the son of Jephunneh Hebron for an inheritance. Hebron therefore became the inheritance of Caleb the son of Jephunneh the Kenezite unto this day, because that he wholly followed the LORD God of Israel. And the name of Hebron before was Kirjath-arba; which Arba was a great man among the Anakims. And the land had rest from war.

There is something very stirring in this record. Caleb, as we know, was one of the two spies who brought back a minority report when the ten spies discouraged the people of Israel. The ten admitted that the land was all God said it would be, and the grapes of Eschol bore witness to its fruitfulness, but they were terrified as they beheld the walled cities and the sons of Anak, mighty giants, in whose sight they were but as grasshoppers, and so they declared it would be impossible to overcome these people of Canaan. But Caleb and Joshua brought back a good report, exclaiming, "Let us go up at once, and possess [the land]; for we are well able to overcome it" (Num. 13:30).

But the people refused to listen and so, as we know, were turned back into the wilderness, there to wander until all that generation, except Caleb and Joshua, had passed away. Now their children had entered into and taken possession of the land. Caleb, though eighty-five years of age, came to Joshua to remind him of the promise that Moses had made, that because he had wholly followed the Lord he should have whatever inheritance his heart desired. He did not look about for some secluded valley where he would be safe from the prying eyes of enemies, nor did he ask for some town or village from which the Canaanites had been driven out already, but he requested Joshua to give him the mountain on which Kirjath-arba was located. Arba was a great man among the Anakims. Kirjath-arba meant the City of Arba. The Anakims still dwelt there, but strong in faith Caleb declared: "If so be the LORD will be with me, then I shall be able to drive them out, as the LORD said." Acting upon Caleb's request, Joshua blessed him and gave him the hill for which he asked as his inheritance. Caleb took possession of it, drove the Anakims out of the city and changed its name to *Hebron*, a word that means "fellowship or communion." The name *Caleb* means "wholehearted" and aptly describes this doughty warrior and faithful servant of God. He did not immediately get possession of Hebron, but he fought stubbornly and determinedly until he had driven out the ancient inhabitants and so took possession of it. Later it became a Levitical city and a city of refuge, but the suburbs belonged to Caleb and his descendants.

As we contemplate this ancient record it should surely stir our hearts and lead us to act as Caleb did—in the energy of faith taking possession of that which God has declared He has given to us in

Christ. No foe can withstand the man of God who presses forward in power of the Spirit and in obedience to the Word.

An old hymn says,

> Faith, mighty faith, the promise sees,
> And looks to that alone;
> Laughs at impossibilities,
> And cries, "It shall be done!"
> —Charles Wesley
> "Father of Jesus Christ, My Lord"

Such a faith was Caleb's and in this he is an example for us all. We are too apt to take the line of least resistance, to be content with that which seems the easiest thing instead of valiantly going on in faith to lay hold of the best that God has for us, no matter what difficulties may seem to make it impossible for us to overcome the foe and to enter into and enjoy our allotted portion.

CHAPTER 14

THE INHERITANCE OF THE TRIBES AND THE STORY OF OTHNIEL AND ACHSAH

Joshua 15–19

We come now to a portion of the book of Joshua which, while it would richly repay careful and minute examination, we must pass over cursorily because of the nature of these messages. In chapters 15–19 we have the account of the division of the land west of the Jordan among the nine and one-half tribes that had not chosen to remain in the country of Bashan and the land of Gilead on the east side of the river, as had the two and one-half tribes, who found there such fine accommodation for pasturing their great herds of cattle. They preferred to settle down in the countries taken from Og, king of Bashan, and Sihon, king of the Amorites, and Moses gave them that permission, as we have seen, providing their warriors went into the land to help their brethren against the Canaanites.

The tribe of Judah had the first portion. Their inheritance was in the high country, adjacent to, and south and west of Jerusalem. Judah was the royal tribe and was honored of God in a very special way, but the other tribes also had their portion in different parts of the land, each one having its own particular values, but divided by the casting of lots. In the book of Proverbs we read, "The lot is cast into the lap; but the whole disposing thereof is of the LORD" (16:33). He directed Joshua to use this method, doubtless in order to avoid what might have seemed like partiality in giving the tribes their inheritances. That there are great spiritual lessons to be learned from these records there can be no question. Others have gone into this in a way we do not attempt here, notably, God's honored servant, F. W. Grant, who in his enlightening notes on these passages in the *Numerical Bible* has shown that the Hebrew names of the cities, towns, and districts all have remarkable significance, and when translated help us to understand more fully something of the richness and preciousness of our inheritance in the heavenly places in Christ. We need to remember that "all these things were written for our learning" and are types of what God has given us to enjoy in this present age of grace.

It is pathetic, however, to note that tribe after tribe failed to make a full end of their enemies and so were obliged to permit these Canaanites to dwell among the Israelites. All this was but a compromise and compromise with evil never pays. In days to come, these foes who had been spared when they should have been exterminated, either became a snare to the people of God by leading them off into idolatry, or else wrought great havoc by their warlike behavior, attacking and often destroying cities and farms of the Israelites who had permitted them to remain unmolested among them. God had warned Israel of this beforehand, telling them that those who were not destroyed would be thorns in their sides and would cause them untold trouble.

Concerning Judah we read in 15:63: "As for the Jebusites the inhabitants of Jerusalem, the children of Judah could not drive them out: but the Jebusites dwell with the children of Judah at Jerusalem unto this day."

Then in 16:10, we learn that the children of Joseph "drave not out the Canaanites that dwelt in Gezer: but the Canaanites dwell among the Ephraimites unto this day, and serve under tribute."

Of Manasseh, the children of the elder son of Joseph, we are told that they "could not drive out the inhabitants of those cities; but the Canaanites would dwell in that land. Yet it came to pass, when the children of Israel were waxen strong, that they put the Canaanites to tribute; but did not utterly drive them out" (17:12–13).

In spite of their failure, we find these children of Joseph grumbling because they had only one lot and one portion to inherit; whereas they declared they were "a great people"! Joshua's answer was fitting indeed: "If thou be a great people, then get thee up to the wood country, and cut down for thyself there in the land of the Perizzites, and of the giants, if mount Ephraim be too narrow for thee" (17:15).

Still these children of Joseph were not satisfied, but they replied: "The hill is not enough for us: and all the Canaanites that dwell in the land of the valley have chariots of iron, both they who are of Beth-shean and her towns, and they who are of the valley of Jezreel" (17:16).

To this Joshua answered somewhat ironically perhaps: "Thou art a great people, and hast great power: thou shalt not have one lot only: but the mountain shall be thine; for it is a wood, and thou shalt cut it down: and the outgoings of it shall be thine: for thou shalt drive out the Canaanites, though they have iron chariots, and though they be strong" (17:17–18).

We may well learn from the failures of Israel to beware lest we ourselves fail to judge every evil thing that Satan would use to hinder our enjoyment of the things of Christ. We are called to deal unsparingly with every unholy thought and every sinful tendency, cleansing ourselves from "all filthiness of the flesh and spirit, perfecting holiness in the fear of God" (2 Cor. 7:1). It is only thus that we can appreciate truly and enjoy, in the way God would have us, the great privileges and manifold blessings He has bestowed upon us. Sin unjudged results in weakness and loss of communion, which can only be restored as we face the sin in the presence of God, confessing and forsaking it, and thus obtaining mercy and the assurance that all is forgiven.

But now let us turn back and consider briefly an incident that shines out brightly in the midst of all these long lists of Hebrew names, which to many of us seem unintelligible. We have already considered the energy of faith as seen in Caleb, the wholehearted. He comes before us again in the thirteenth verse of chapter 15, where we read:

> And unto Caleb the son of Jephunneh he gave a part among
> the children of Judah, according to the commandment of the
> LORD to Joshua, even the city of Arba the father of Anak,

which city is Hebron. And Caleb drove thence the three sons of Anak, Sheshai, and Ahiman, and Talmai, the children of Anak. And he went up thence to the inhabitants of Debir: and the name of Debir before was Kirjath-sepher. (vv. 13–15)

Kirjath-sepher means "the city of the book." It was probably so named because an ancient library was located there. Its name was changed later to *Debir*, which means "the oracle or the word," and suggests that Word of God through which He speaks directly to His people. Caleb's energy set a splendid example to younger men and this comes out clearly in what follows. We are told in verse 16: "And Caleb said, He that smiteth Kirjath-sepher, and taketh it, to him will I give Achsah my daughter to wife."

Achsah means "anklet," and, as others have suggested, speaks of the decorated foot, reminding us of the word in the prophecy of Isaiah, "How beautiful upon the mountains are the feet of him that bringeth good tidings, that publisheth peace" (52:7). In Ephesians 6:15 the soldier of Christ is commanded to have his "feet shod with the preparation of the gospel of peace." Surely, no lovelier decoration could be found for any foot than this.

In response to Caleb's challenge, we are told that Othniel, his nephew, took Kirjath-sepher, and thus the city of the book, or the word, became his inheritance. In accordance with his promise, Caleb gave him Achsah to be his wife. Thus the cousins were united. Achsah suggested to her husband that he ask of her father a field, a petition which Caleb readily granted, but the young woman realized that a field without water was practically worthless; so she herself approached her father in an attitude of supplication. In response to his inquiry, "What wouldest thou?" she replied, "Give me a blessing; for thou hast given me a south land; give me also springs of water" (15:18–19).

We are told that Caleb gave her the upper springs and the nether springs. This is all very suggestive. A believer may have rich treasure indeed in the fact that the oracles of God are committed to him, but he can only enjoy to the full this blessed gift of God when the Holy Spirit is given in power to open up the truth to him. In this dispensation of grace the Spirit dwells in every believer. He is likened by our Lord Jesus to a fountain of living water springing up in the heart. It is as we appreciate and value the work of the Holy Spirit that we enjoy the refreshing influences which flow from His acknowledged presence. May the faith of Othniel and of Achsah be duplicated in us, who through grace have been blessed with all spiritual blessings in heavenly places in Christ. May we be so yielded to the indwelling Holy Spirit that He will make very real to us the precious things of Christ, and thus give us to enjoy our inheritance to the full. The Spirit and the Word are linked together, both in connection with the new birth and in later Christian experience. The Spirit-filled believer is one in whom the Word of Christ dwells richly. May this be true of all who read these lines!

CHAPTER 15

THE CITIES OF REFUGE

Joshua 20

It is very evident that God has hidden some special lessons for us in the types of the City of Refuge, of which we now read in chapter 20, as otherwise we would find ourselves wondering why they are mentioned so frequently. In four previous passages the Spirit of God drew the attention of Israel to the importance of these cities and the expression of His grace toward the unwitting or unintentional manslayer in Israel. First, we have the brief intimation in Exodus 21:13, telling Israel that when they reached the land, God would provide such a refuge: "And if a man lie not in wait, but God deliver him into his hand; then I will appoint thee a place whither he shall flee." Then we have much fuller information in Numbers 35:6, 9–28:

And among the cities which ye shall give unto the Levites there shall be six cities for refuge, which ye shall appoint for the manslayer, that he may flee thither: and to them ye shall add forty and two cities. . . .

And the LORD spake unto Moses, saying, Speak unto the children of Israel, and say unto them, When ye be come over Jordan into the land of Canaan; then ye shall appoint you cities to be cities of refuge for you; that the slayer may flee thither, which killeth any person at unawares. And they shall be unto you cities for refuge from the avenger; that the manslayer die not, until he stand before the congregation in judgment. And of these cities which ye shall give six cities shall ye have for refuge. Ye shall give three cities on this side Jordan, and three cities shall ye give in the land of Canaan, which shall be cities of refuge. These six cities shall be a refuge, both for the children of Israel, and for the stranger, and for the sojourner among them: that every one that killeth any person unawares may flee thither. And if he smite him with an instrument of iron, so that he die, he is a murderer: the murderer shall surely be put to death. And if he smite him with throwing a stone, wherewith he may die, and he die, he is a murderer: the murderer shall surely be put to death. Or if he smite him with an handweapon of wood, wherewith he may die, and he die, he is a murderer: the murderer shall surely be put to death. The revenger of blood himself shall slay the murderer: when he meeteth him, he shall slay him. But if he thrust him of hatred, or hurl at him by laying of wait, that he die; or in enmity smite him with his hand, that he die: he that smote him shall surely be put to death; for he is a murderer: the revenger of blood shall slay the murderer, when he meeteth him. But if he thrust him suddenly without enmity, or have cast upon him any thing without laying of wait, or with any stone, wherewith a man may die, seeing him not, and cast it upon him, that he die, and was not his enemy, neither sought his harm: then the congregation shall judge between the slayer and the revenger of blood according to these judgments: and the congregation shall deliver the slayer out of the hand of the revenger of blood, and the congregation shall restore him to the city of his refuge, whither he was fled: and he shall abide in it unto the death of the high priest, which was anointed with the holy oil. But if the slayer shall at any time come without the border of the city of his refuge, whither he was fled; and the revenger of blood find him without the borders of the city of his refuge, and the revenger of blood kill the slayer; he shall not be guilty of blood: because he should have remained in the city of his refuge until the death of the high priest: but after the death of the high priest the slayer shall return into the land of his possession.

It is perhaps hardly necessary for our purpose to quote the remaining passages, both of which are found in the book of Deuteronomy, namely, 4:41–43 and 19:1–10. With these Scriptures our present chapter is in perfect harmony. It gives us the complete fulfillment of God's command concerning these cities of refuge, of which there were six in all: three on the east of Jordan and three on the west. Clear, open roads were to be kept leading from all parts of the land to one or other of these cities, with definite signs indicating the nearest one, so that the man who had slain another in Israel without hating him in his heart or intending to kill him, might flee at once to the city of refuge and so be protected from the avenger of blood.

It is important to observe that there was no refuge offered to the one who was guilty of deliberate and willful murder. God had declared, "Ye shall take no satisfaction for the life of a murderer" (Num. 35:31), but for the manslayer there was ever the open gate in order that he might be secure from the vengeance of the relatives of the one he had killed. When we come over to the New Testament we read in Hebrews 6:18 of those "who have fled for refuge to lay hold upon the hope set before [them]." The reference is to those who, though conscious of their own sinfulness have availed themselves of the salvation procured for them by our Lord Jesus Christ upon the cross. All who find a refuge in Him are safe forever from the judgment of a Holy God. But if He be rejected after the gospel has been clearly proclaimed, and men deliberately crucify to themselves the Son of God afresh, putting Him to an open shame, there is for them no hope of deliverance. Christ rejected means eternal judgment.

The whole world, Jew and Gentile, stands guilty before God as having participated in that which brought about the death of His Son, but inasmuch as Christ came to give Himself a ransom for all, His sacrifice on the cross has opened up, as it were, a city of refuge for all who put their trust in Him.

Of old, the manslayer was to remain in the city of refuge until the death of the high priest. Christ is not only the Man slain and the city of refuge Himself, but He too is the High Priest, and as such He will never die again. His is an everlasting priesthood; so those who find refuge in Him are eternally saved.

> Once in Him [Christ], in Him [Christ] for ever,
> Thus the eternal covenant stands.
>
> —John Kent
> "Sovereign Grace o'er Sin Abounding"

He settled the sin question on the cross and He put all mankind on the ground of manslaughter instead of murder when He prayed for those who had been so active in rejecting Him, and even in nailing Him to the cross, "Father, forgive them; for they know not what they do" (Luke 23:34). In other words, the Father might consider them guilty of the sin of ignorance or unintentional manslaughter rather than the willful murder of the Son of God.

The apostle Peter in addressing the Jews shortly after Pentecost, said: "And now, brethren, I wot that through ignorance ye did it, as did also your rulers. But those things, which God before had shown by the mouth of all his prophets, that Christ should suffer, he hath so fulfilled" (Acts 3:17–18). And in view of this Peter called upon them to repent, saying: "Repent ye therefore, and be converted, that your sins may be blotted out, when the times of refreshing shall come from the presence of the Lord; and he shall send Jesus Christ, which before was preached unto you: whom the heaven must receive until the times of restitution of all things, which God hath spoken by the mouth of all his holy prophets since the world began" (Acts 3:19–21).

The apostle Paul emphasizes the same thing when in 1 Corinthians 2:6–8, he says:

Howbeit we speak wisdom among them that are perfect: yet not the wisdom of this world, nor of the princes of this world, that come to nought: but we speak the wisdom of God in a mystery, even the hidden wisdom, which God ordained before the world unto our glory: which none of the princes of this world knew: for had they known it, they would not have crucified the Lord of glory.

According to these passages God looks upon the whole world as guilty of the sin of manslaughter in connection with the death of Christ, but has opened up a new and living way into the place of refuge for all who go to Him, confessing their sins and thus availing themselves of His grace. What folly, then, for men to turn a deaf ear to the call of God and to persist in the rejection of the salvation He offers them!

We have an outstanding example in the Old Testament of a man who was slain just outside the wall of a city of refuge, who would have been safe inside. I refer to Abner, of whom David lamented, crying, "Died Abner as a fool dieth?" (2 Sam. 3:33). With no malice aforethought on his part, Abner had slain Asahel, the brother of Joab. Abiding in the city of refuge, he would have been secure from the avenger of blood, but Joab found him outside the city and put him to death in retaliation for the killing of Asahel.

What fools men are who now deliberately refuse the security that God offers in Christ Himself, and so by spurning Him become guilty before God of the murder of His Son.

It would seem as though the names of the six cities of refuge have suggestive meaning, at least, they may well bring to our minds some of the privileges that are ours in Christ. The three cities on the western side of the Jordan were Kedesh in Galilee, Shechem in Mt. Ephraim, and Hebron in the mountains of Judah. On the other side of Jordan the three selected were Bezer in the tribe of Reuben, Ramoth in Gilead, and Golan in Bashan.

Kedesh is "the sanctuary" and it is in Christ Himself that the troubled soul finds sanctuary in the midst of a world of strife and sin. *Shechem* means "a shoulder," when our blessed Lord is said to carry the government of the world on His shoulder (Isa. 9) and the Good Shepherd places the sheep that was lost upon His shoulders. And so all believers are sustained by Him, who is our strength and who undertakes to carry us safely through all the trials of life. *Hebron* means "communion" and suggests that precious fellowship with Christ into which believers are brought through Christ.

The names of the cities on the east of Jordan would seem to be definitely significant, although the meaning of some of them is a little uncertain. *Bezer* is said to come from a root meaning "munitions or fortress," and may speak to us of Christ Himself, who is for all who believe a strong tower and fort of security. *Ramoth* is generally understood as meaning "the heights," and may be an intimation of the precious truth that God has raised us up together and seated us together in the heavenlies in Christ. *Golan* is perhaps the most uncertain of all, but one meaning given to it is "their rejoicing," which may remind us that "the joy of the Lord is our strength."

In obedience to the Word of God, given so long before, Joshua set aside these cities of refuge, each one of them a Levitical city and each one with an open door to receive the poor, distressed soul who is fleeing from the avenger of blood. Looked at individually or corporately, they all tell us of Him who is our refuge and strength, our Savior from judgment.

> In the refuge God provided,
> Though the world's destruction lowers,
> We are safe to Christ confided;
> Everlasting life is ours.
> —Mary Bowley

CHAPTER 16

THE LAST DAYS OF JOSHUA'S LEADERSHIP

Joshua 21–24

We may consider these closing chapters of the book of Joshua as a group, as the matters with which they deal are all so intimately linked together. In chapter 21 we read of the separation of forty-eight cities from among the various tribes of Israel, which were allotted to the Levites. In chapter 22 we get the return of the warriors of the two-and-a-half tribes to the homes which had already been given to them by Moses on the east of the Jordan. In chapters 23 and 24 we listen to Joshua as he seeks solemnly to impress upon the nation, which he had led into the possession of the land, the importance of cleaving closely to the Word of the Lord and not being turned aside through following any of the customs of the surrounding nations.

The Levites, as we know, were not to be numbered among the people of Israel; therefore they did not inherit any special portion of the land of Palestine. They had been chosen by God instead of the firstborn, who were dedicated to Him because of the deliverance wrought on the Passover night in Egypt and were set apart for special service in connection with the sanctuary and also ministering and teaching the Word of God among the people. The Lord Himself was their portion and their inheritance. So long as the people were obedient to Him, the Levites would be well cared for. In after years, when the nation drifted away from God, the Levites suffered greatly and in many instances were obliged to forsake the special service committed to them in order to care for their fields and vineyards, that they might properly provide for their families and themselves. Of old, God's people were divided into three classes: priests, Levites, and warriors. The priests were the worshipers and had to do with the way of approach to God. The Levites were the ministers of the Lord, serving, as we have seen, in various capacities. The warriors fought to take possession of the land and to hold it against their enemies in days to come. In the present dispensation of grace, the three groups are combined in each believer. All have been set apart of God as priests, holy and royal, to offer unto God spiritual sacrifices and to make known the riches of His grace to a lost world. All are Levites, whose joy it should be to serve with gladness the One who has redeemed them. All, too, are warriors, responsible to contend earnestly for the faith once for all committed to the saints.

Cities, with their suburbs, were set apart for the possession of the Levites throughout the entire land, taken from the inheritances of the various tribes. Thus it was the privilege of all to share with the servants of the Lord that which He had given them and which they had appropriated in faith. This provision for the Levites was made after the Lord had given Israel all the land which He swore to give unto their fathers, and they possessed it and dwelt therein. God had fulfilled his Word to the letter. It was now the responsibility of His people to hold by obedience that which they had inherited.

In chapter 22 we learn that these warriors had done their part faithfully (vv. 1–6). Although they speak of those who prefer to settle down on the borders of the world rather than to enter in and possess in fullness all that God has for them, nevertheless, according to the light which they seemed to have, they were true and faithful to the promise they had given to Moses and so they were now entitled to return to Bashan and Gilead and adjoining districts east of the Jordan to settle down with their families and care for their flocks and herds.

On their way to their homes an incident occurred which is very suggestive and might well be kept in mind by us today—we who are so apt to misunderstand one another's motives and to judge each other wrongly because we do not know what is going on in the heart. It is against this that our Lord warns us when He says, "Judge not, that ye be not judged. For with what judgment ye judge, ye shall be judged: and with what measure ye mete, it shall be measured to you" (Matt. 7:1–2).

In Joshua 22:10 we read:

And when they came unto the borders of Jordan, that are in the land of Canaan, the children of Reuben and the children of Gad and the half tribe of Manasseh built there an altar by Jordan, a great altar to see to.

When word got abroad regarding the building of this altar, those who had their inheritances west of the Jordan immediately jumped at the conclusion that their brethren were setting up some separate kind of worship and so were making a breach in Israel. Without sending messengers to make proper inquiry, word was sent to all the nine and one-half tribes that a rebellion against the Word of the Lord had begun and they were summoned together to quell it. Led by that devoted man Phineas, the son of Eleazar the priest, they charged their brethren with trespass against the Lord, and reminding them how judgment had fallen upon them because of previous iniquities, they warned them of what they might expect if they continued to rebel against God by setting up some other center of worship than that which He had already established at Shiloh. But when thus charged by their excited brethren, the two and one-half tribes, through their leader, made it clear that they had no such thought whatever.

On the other hand, the altar they had built was in order to remind their children and the children of the nine-and-one-half tribes that they were one nation and that together they worshipped the one true and living God. When the facts of the case came out clearly, Phineas and the host following him were satisfied, and they thanked God that division was averted. The altar that the children of Reuben and of Gad had built was simply a replica of that which was set up at the tabernacle and was designed to keep in mind the unity of the nation rather than to foment division. Thus what might have been a very serious breach between brethren was avoided. How often through the centuries have Christians attacked one another and separated one from another on even less provocation, simply because they acted in haste and did not take time to acquaint themselves with one another's motives!

As we turn to chapter 23 we read:

> And it came to pass a long time after that the LORD had given rest unto Israel from all their enemies round about, that Joshua waxed old and stricken in age. And Joshua called for all Israel, and for their elders, and for their heads, and for their judges, and for their officers, and said unto them, I am old and stricken in age: and ye have seen all that the LORD your God hath done unto all these nations because of you; for the LORD your God is he that hath fought for you. (vv. 1–3)

Joshua then went on to remind them how he had divided the land by lot among them and how the Lord their God had expelled their enemies in the past. If they continued to walk in obedience He could be depended on to drive out those that remained, in order that Israel might possess the land in peace and quietness, even as God had promised them. It was for them to be courageous and obedient and to seek to walk in all the commandments of the Lord, as set forth in the law of Moses. Then they could depend upon God to keep His Word and act on their behalf. If, on the other hand, they failed in this and did not cleave to the Lord their God, but turned from His law to walk in the ways of the nations surrounding Palestine or of the remnant of those remaining in the land, then their own God would turn against them and they would learn in bitterness of soul the folly of disobedience to His truth.

> And, behold, this day I am going the way of all the earth:
> and ye know in all your hearts and in all your souls, that
> not one thing hath failed of all the good things which the
> LORD your God spake concerning you; all are come to pass
> unto you, and not one thing hath failed thereof. Therefore
> it shall come to pass, that as all good things are come upon
> you, which the LORD your God promised you; so shall the
> LORD bring upon you all evil things, until he have destroyed
> you from off this good land which the LORD your God hath
> given you. When ye have transgressed the covenant of the
> LORD your God, which he commanded you, and have gone
> and served other gods, and bowed yourselves to them; then
> shall the anger of the LORD be kindled against you, and ye
> shall perish quickly from off the good land which he hath
> given unto you. (23:14–16)

Following this, Joshua now an aged man, gathered all the tribes
of Israel to Shechem to give them his last charge. He reminded them
how God had called Abraham from Mesopotamia and set him apart,
that through him all nations of the world might be blessed.

It is evident from chapter 24, verse 2, that Abraham himself had
been brought up in idolatry and belonged to an idolatrous family at
the time that God revealed Himself to him. Joshua said,

> Your fathers dwelt on the other side of the flood [that is, of the
> river Euphrates] in old time, even Terah, the father of Abra-
> ham, and the father of Nachor: and they served other gods.

Abraham was not called out from the nations because he was
inherently different from other people, but God in His sovereignty

chose him from an idolatrous family and revealed Himself to him. They were His children. They knew how wonderfully the Lord had fulfilled His word to their fathers, and now they were responsible to yield implicit obedience to His word. Joshua recited briefly an account of God's dealings with them under Moses in Egypt and in the wilderness, and then reminded them of recent events after they entered into the land. Everything Jehovah had promised was fulfilled. He had given them the land for which they had not labored and cities which they did not build. In these they dwelt securely with the vineyards and the olive yards which they had not planted but of which they ate. They were responsible, therefore, to "fear the LORD, and serve him in sincerity and in truth: and put away the gods which your fathers served on the other side of the flood, and in Egypt; and serve ye the LORD" (24:14).

This is very illuminating and shows us that even in Egypt idolatry had a hold on some in Israel, even as we know was true in the wilderness, and now that they were settled in the land there were still idols to be brought out into the light and destroyed. So long as anything is given the place in our hearts that belongs to God Himself, there can never be the fullness of blessing that He would have us enjoy.

Joshua's own steadfast purpose is emphasized in 24:15. After calling upon Israel to choose at once whom they would serve, whether Baal or Jehovah, he declares, "As for me and my house, we will serve the LORD."

For the doughty old warrior who had seen so much of the mighty acts of the one true and living God there could be no thought of any other god. Nor would he allow for one moment that those subject to his headship in the family relation should take any other course. Jehovah was his God and the God of his household. His was an unflinching and unquestioning loyalty to the Holy One of Israel whom he had served for so long.

Responding to Joshua's words, we are told in 24:16–18:

> And the people answered and said, God forbid that we should forsake the LORD, to serve other gods; for the LORD our God, he it is that brought us up and our fathers out of the land of Egypt, from the house of bondage, and which did those great signs in our sight, and preserved us in all the way wherein we went, and among all the people through whom we passed: and the LORD drave out from before us all the people, even the Amorites which dwelt in the land: therefore will we also serve the LORD; for he is our God.

All this sounded very good and no doubt at the moment those who made such protestations of loyalty to Joshua meant every word they uttered. But time was to prove how untrustworthy the human heart is. Joshua realized it and warned the people accordingly, as we read in 24:19–20:

> And Joshua said unto the people, Ye cannot serve the LORD: for he is an holy God; he is a jealous God; he will not forgive your transgressions nor your sins. If ye forsake the LORD, and serve strange gods, then he will turn and do you hurt, and consume you, after that he hath done you good.

However, the people replied, "Nay; but we will serve the LORD" (24:21). And God called Joshua to witness against them that they had thus confirmed their devotion to Him. Again the command came: "Now therefore put away, said he, the strange gods which are among you, and incline your heart unto the LORD God of Israel" (24:23).

The people protested their full intention to be obedient. So we are told,

> Joshua made a covenant with the people that day, and set them a statute and an ordinance in Shechem. And Joshua wrote these words in the book of the law of God, and took a great stone, and set it up there under an oak, that was by the sanctuary of the LORD. And Joshua said unto all the people, Behold, this stone shall be a witness unto us; for it hath heard all the words of the LORD which he spake unto us: it shall be therefore a witness unto you, lest ye deny your God. (vv. 25–27)

After such solemn adjuration the people departed to their homes.

The death of Joshua followed shortly after, and he was buried in the borders of his inheritance in Timnath-serah.

In 24:31 we learn that "Israel served the LORD all the days of Joshua, and all the days of the elders that overlived Joshua, and which had known all the works of the LORD, that he had done for Israel." The history that follows in later books tells us how terribly the people failed to carry out their part of the covenant which the fathers had made.

One thing remains to be noticed ere we close our present study of this book. We read in 24:32:

And the bones of Joseph, which the children of Israel brought up out of Egypt, buried they in Shechem, in a parcel of ground which Jacob bought of the sons of Hamor the father of Shechem for an hundred pieces of silver: and it became the inheritance of the children of Joseph.

Before Joseph died, by faith he gave commandment concerning his bones, exhorting his brethren not to allow his embalmed body to remain in the land of Egypt, but to carry it with them to Canaan and bury it there. So when Moses led the people out of Egypt, we are told he took the bones of Joseph with him. All through the forty years in the wilderness when they were bearing about in the body the dying of Joseph, the memorial of death, the death of the one who had been used of God for their deliverance, who might be described as their Savior, was with them. Now that all had been fulfilled and they were settled in the land, they buried the bones of Joseph in the parcel of ground which he himself had indicated.

May we not learn from this the importance of always bearing about in the body the dying of the Lord Jesus, that the life also of Jesus might be manifested in us until that day when, the wilderness journey ended, we shall enter into our final rest in the paradise of God above.